How America
Goes to War

How America Goes to War

Frank E. Vandiver

Modern Military Tradition
Jon L. Wakelyn, Series Editor

Westport, Connecticut
London

Library of Congress Cataloging-in-Publication Data

Vandiver, Frank Everson, 1925–
    How America goes to war / Frank E. Vandiver.
      p. cm.—(Modern military tradition)
    Includes bibliographical references and index.
    ISBN 0–275–98514–8 (alk. paper)
    1. United States—History, Military. 2. War and emergency powers—
United States—History. I. Title. II. Series.
    E181.V36 2005
    355'.033073'09—dc22   2005004212

British Library Cataloguing in Publication Data is available.

Library of Congress Catalog Card Number: 2005004212
ISBN: 0–275–98514–8
ISSN: 1553–7196

First published in 2005

Praeger Publishers, 88 Post Road West, Westport, CT 06881
An imprint of Greenwood Publishing Group, Inc.
www.praeger.com

Printed in the United States of America

The paper used in this book complies with the
Permanent Paper Standard issued by the National
Information Standards Organization (Z39.48–1984).

10 9 8 7 6 5 4 3 2 1

No protracted war can fail to endanger the freedom of a democratic country. . . . War does not always give over democratic communities to military government, but it must invariably increase the powers of civil government. All those who seek to destroy the liberties of a democratic nation ought to know that war is the surest and the shortest means to accomplish it.

—Alexis de Tocqueville, *Democracy in America*

Contents

Foreword

Frank E. Vandiver passed away just after he delivered the finished text of this important work in military history to the publisher. A pioneer in the study of warfare and warriors, from his earliest work Vandiver understood the relationship between preparedness and the ability to fight. His book on Josiah Gorgas remains a landmark effort on the value of logistics in warfare. The countless articles and thematic books he wrote on the Civil War revealed to his peers his nearly effortless powers to describe men and their materiel of war. His *Mighty Stonewall* was the first work to reveal how that great captain Thomas J. Jackson prepared for and fought an offensive war. Vandiver, always keen on the comparative dimension in war studies, next wrote the definitive biography of that great student of modern warfare, Black Jack Pershing. Vandiver's love of the Great War, and his time spent as Harmsworth Professor at Oxford, led to an enduring interest in the career of Field Marshal Douglas Haig, about whom he had long planned to write a biography.

Generations of readers and Vandiver's many students benefitted from both his work and his many friendships. From his first students at Washington University, to a generation of students trained at Rice University, to the gifted students he somehow managed to take on while serving as a dynamic president of Texas A&M, to his splendid mentoring of scholars at the Mosher Institute for International Policy Studies, all who have come under his tutelage have sung his praises.

This book, perhaps his last work, continued Vandiver's quest to understand the relationship of warfare to society and its institutional life. In it he has clarified brilliantly how a democratic republic fails to prepare to defend itself, then through its military talent rallies the people to fight in their own behalf. In this bold work Vandiver assesses our military actions from our origins as a revolutionary republic to a twenty-first century country fighting to defend and to expand freedom. Vandiver well understands the technology of warfare, the science of making weapons for fighting, the ability to deliver military personnel and materiel to the front lines, and the genius of leadership. With great sadness over his passing, but with great pride, we deliver this volume to those who wish to understand why and how their country goes to war.

Jon Wakelyn

Preface

When President George W. Bush launched the war against terrorism I became interested in how America has gotten into its wars. I could find no single tome to tell the story and began digging for information. Looking at conflicts after independence, I found that trends were various—but it quickly seemed clear that Congress has generally abandoned its constitutional war declaration power as increasingly belligerent presidents have expanded their role as commanders-in-chief. James K. Polk involved the United States in war with Mexico, and Congress reluctantly supported him. Several chief executives have scattered Marines around the Caribbean to enforce the Monroe Doctrine, to keep peace, to prop up friendly governments and topple unfriendly ones.

Going to war is a complex venture for a democracy, as de Tocqueville noted. Once in, all kinds of laws go into effect to strengthen the government's power to wage war, to control the flow and use of money, to turn civilians into soldiers, hasten war manufactures, suppress sedition, and make pro-war propaganda the truth of the day. All of which means that the political structure of the nation shifts as regimentation supplants freedom. Emotions and politics have sometimes dictated America's belligerency, especially in some of the Indian wars and the Civil War. Domestic opinion is sometimes shaped (and warped) by propaganda into serious errors of national judgment, even into unjustifiable conflicts. With such painful results obvious, I wondered how going to war seemed to get easier with experience, how the United States shifted from peace loving to war making. I wondered, too, if an "American way of war" developed and, if so, how, and into what? From the many small wars America fought, what lessons were learned from the wages of success? Did America become more or less democratic, more or less belligerent, or, perhaps tragically, a bulking imperium?

As wars got bigger and the world more complicated in the twentieth century, presidents got bolder. John F. Kennedy skated the edges of nuclear war during the Cuban missile crisis without telling Congress how bad things were with the Soviet Union. He followed President Eisenhower's lead in sending advisers to South Vietnam, and Lyndon Johnson used a Tonkin Gulf encounter as a new way of going all the way to conflict—via the Tonkin Gulf Resolution that gave him carte blanche to send troops to Asia. Harry Truman used the UN charter to get around Congress, as did George H. W. Bush before the Persian Gulf War. After the terrorist attacks on September 11, 2001, the second President Bush secured another permissive resolution from a frightened Congress. The resolution idea is interesting. Since the Constitution gives Congress the power to declare war but is silent on how Congress may do that, general resolutions permitting conflicts are probably entirely acceptable.

Congress formally declared war twice in the twentieth century—World Wars I and II—but somewhat reluctantly supported "our troops" in Korea, in Grenada, and in the varied UN Balkan ventures. Attempting to recapture its authority, Congress passed the War Powers Resolution in 1973, which is condemned by most presidents and honored mainly by evasion.

Specifics of getting into war led me on to collateral interests, particularly how each American conflict built upon previous ones to change the way the United States defended its growing imperialism. President Eisenhower warned of the "military-industrial complex," but without close collaboration among industry, money, and brains, the nation would probably not be the surviving superpower. So the book grew beyond war beginnings to a look at what the wars accomplished, how they escalated, and how they eventually influenced foreign policy.

Many people have helped with this book. Special gratitude to Lt. Gen. Dave Palmer (U.S. Army, Ret.), who helped define wars for me. My lasting thanks, always, to my wife, Renée, who scanned the manuscript with a close eye and prevented some embarrassing errors. I owe my matchless research assistant, Edith Anderson Wakefield, a debt beyond repayment.

She searched for references, scoured the Internet, plumbed the Interlibrary Loan network, read and edited the manuscript, and still kept a healthy good humor! Shannon Maxwell Hill, my administrative assistant, kept the office running, tended e-mails, correspondence, and phones, and retyped without rancor—many thanks, Shannon!

My whole family listened to long reaches of prose without visible fatigue. Editor Mary Lenn Dixon of the Texas A&M University Press lent her discerning listening ear and valiantly helped me keep the faith.

Special thanks to my exemplary parents and two sets of great in-laws for all kinds of help. A special thanks, as always, to the Cushing Memorial Library at Texas A&M University for patience and unflagging support.

Jon Wakelyn, friend and editor of this series, has my deepest appreciation for sticking with me, while Heather Staines, Praeger editor, is a model critic and aide. I offer grateful thanks to my agent, Mike Hamilburg, whose counsel kept me on track.

All of the above are absolved of any errors or opinions!

1

The Whiskey Rebellion

A venerable beverage caused the first serious home challenge to the United States government—whiskey. And it is probable that Alexander Hamilton is responsible for the Whiskey Rebellion. In 1791 he pushed through a federal excise tax of 25 percent on whiskey and distilleries. Many farmers beyond the Alleghenies in Pennsylvania, New Jersey, Virginia, and Maryland made the most of their money by converting their grain into whiskey for easier cartage across the mountains. They finally flatly refused to pay the tax—it smacked of an earlier and infamous levy on tea. A good many other people resented it, too, because whiskey served as a kind of barter currency in that remote section where governments were mistrusted. In May 1794 some seventy-five distillers were charged with tax evasion and ordered to Philadelphia for trial.

From simple evasion the "Whiskey Boys" began attacking tax collectors, tarring and feathering some. Shots were fired on July 15, 1794, and on July 17 some five hundred irked distillers burned down an excise inspector's home. Two weeks later, after much arguing, talking, and drinking, the Whiskey Boys marched through Pittsburgh and meandered home. The rebellion fizzled.

Meantime, Secretary of the Treasury Hamilton urged a hard line against the rebellion. There had been earlier uprisings—notably Shays's Rebellion—but both Hamilton and President George Washington saw the whiskey fracas as the first truly serious threat to somewhat shaky federal authority. Determined to carry out his constitutional duty to preserve domestic tranquility and enforce the nation's laws, the president asked Pennsylvania's governor to send the state militia to help the tax collectors. The governor begged off by saying the whole thing was a federal problem—and besides, he did not have enough men. State refusal heightened the threat to national authority.

Aware that he had direct authority to act under Article II of the Constitution, which ordered the president to "take care that the Laws be faithfully executed," Washington walked a cautious trail in attacking domestic insurrection. A complication: he would have to use militia since General Anthony Wayne had the regulars fighting Indians in the Northwest Territory. The president had sound legal grounds to federalize the militia under a congressional act of 1792, but since this would be the first time the act was invoked, there was some doubt whether militiamen would shoot at fellow Americans or fellow militiamen.

In calling for militia quotas from Pennsylvania, Virginia, New Jersey, and Maryland, Washington stuck strictly to his congressional mandate. First he got Associate Justice of the Supreme Court James Wilson (whose private practice had been in Pennsylvania) to certify that in southwestern Pennsylvania "laws of the United States are opposed and the execution thereof obstructed by combinations too powerful to be suppressed by the ordinary course of judicial proceedings or by the powers vested in the marshal."[1] Washington issued an August 1794 proclamation calling for militia. He did it reluctantly, he said, and because "the essential interests of the Union demand it, that the very existence of government and the fundamental principles of social order are materially involved in acts of treason."[2]

Trouble dogged gathering the militias. Sympathy for the Whiskey Boys of Pennsylvania bubbled in western Maryland—Governor Thomas Lee had to deal with a small revolt in his state's western areas that threatened an arsenal in Frederick. Virginia governor "Light Horse Harry" Lee met similar disenchantment. New Jersey's governor, Richard Howell, did better—he had an efficient militia system that worked without problems. Governor Thomas Mifflin of Pennsylvania had the hardest job; he finally made heroic efforts but could not raise his whole quota.

All the state chief executives faced daunting supply problems as men slowly mobilized. Getting a force of some 14,000 across the mountains depended on large stores of food, ammunition, arms, powder, and clothing—all the miscellany of hard campaigning. Only New Jersey boasted

George Washington, first president and commander-in-chief (1789–1797). Copy of painting by Gilbert Stuart. Courtesy of NARA, George Washington Bicentennial Commission.

some small supply success. The rest of the states wallowed in a morass of contracting and collecting, badgering and begging. Faced with incipient chaos, the governors of Pennsylvania, New Jersey, and Virginia decided to lead their own troops.

Congress could legislate militia management, but the states had wide latitude. For some time American militiamen (who would finally evolve into the modern National Guard) had suffered the derision of British regulars as well as the slights of their own countrymen. The Constitutional Convention, and several authors of the Federalist Papers, shied away from any kind of United States military force as a threat to liberty. Militias were sought by the states for domestic protection and were, at last, continued—though Congress won the power to "raise and support armies." Militias, even though they could be federalized, and despite their often heroic performance, kept a persisting image as a second class force, lax in officer training and haphazardly supplied.

Disorganization combined with recruiting and logistical delays hardly surprised the president. For years he had inveighed to deaf ears against militia neglect. While the states floundered, Washington acted. Realizing the federal government would have to sustain the troops in the field, he handed supply problems to the energetic Hamilton and turned to the thorny issue of leadership.

A delicate matter—since most governors had Revolutionary War experience, they fancied themselves in command. Washington could use them. He named the gathering force the Army of the Constitution and wanted to show it under civilian control. He asked Light Horse Harry to take charge "if I do not go out myself."[3] Lee jumped at the chance: "My grief for the necessity of pointing the bayonet against the breasts of our countrymen is equaled only by my conviction of the wisdom of your decision to compel immediate submission to the authority of the laws."[4]

On September 25 the president published another proclamation announcing that a large army was "in motion to the scene of disaffection." On September 30 he and Hamilton left for Carlisle, Pennsylvania, and a rendezvous with the army. Hamilton noticed that the general, who had always been a rum drinker, switched to whiskey!

Some old, familiar excitement probably touched the president as he went again to join an army—but at sixty-two Washington knew he lacked the energy, perhaps the boldness, of earlier commands. And, too, he worried still about "the man on the white horse" image that his presence might project. That image would be worsened by having old aide Hamilton along, a man the Republicans and the Whiskey Boys disliked. On October 4, 1794, Washington joined his Army of the Constitution in Carlisle.

Sadly enough, this force looked distressingly like the Continental Army when first he joined it some two decades before. Milling hordes in variegated colors, more an agglomeration than an army, clogged the town. No discipline, chaotic supply problems, misfits, old veterans, dandies, such was the national militia—a rabble nicknamed a "watermelon army." Washington addressed this dismal scene with a revealing order: "It is a[n] . . . important idea that those who are called out in support and defense of the laws, should not give occasion . . . to impute to them infractions of the law."[5] Fortunately good officers were handy to speed organization.

Light Horse Harry whipped the Virginia and Maryland forces into sound shape before Washington saw them, and that convinced the president to give overall command of some eleven thousand men to Lee. Actually, the whole expedition might well have disbanded. Faced with Washington's ire and a gathering punishment, the Whiskey Boys had either gone home or skedaddled to the west. In late October Lee took his men across the mountains in a hideous wintry march and sent some twenty undoubted culprits to Philadelphia for trial. He left a small occupying force behind and dismissed his army.

Important lessons came from this nearly bloodless venture in domestic regulation. Clearly the United States government could protect itself, despite rumors to the contrary; militia, though disorganized, could form armies. The Whiskey Campaign proved again the old military maxim that all campaigns should be fought with overwhelming force. Washington set a precedent for executive action.

Edging Toward Peace

Those who suffered through the birth pangs of Liberty were acutely sensitive to its growing pains. Many Revolutionary patriots chafed at the evidence of lingering British influence in America. Various border issues remained unsettled; some British officers still connived with northwestern Indians about disputed ground; whiffs of snubbery touched trade and diplomatic relations with Perfidious Albion. Especially irksome were the whispers from Canada and the heavily Federalist northeastern states that the weakling American republic could survive only with English help.

All of which tended to increase American admiration for France, itself engulfed in revolution against monarchy. Admiration escalated to adulation, then silly foppery. Finally, the outrages of France's new ambassador to the United States, Citizen Genet—at one party he had beheaded effigies of the dead king and queen parade around the table—sickened Washington. Secretary of State Thomas Jefferson engineered Genet's recall. France further eroded American affection by attacking United States merchant ships. It should be said for France that it was not alone in harassing Yankee shipping—Britain's navy also did its part. War with France pushed England to a European blockade that resulted in a Napoleonic declaration of counter-blockade. Both countries captured neutral ships, levied fines, and imprisoned crews. American ships, numerous and unarmed, suffered the most.

From the mid-1780s attacks and insults escalated. Diplomatic efforts failed to stop the marauding: American ships were captured and American seamen enslaved and held for ransom. At last an exasperated President John Adams called Congress into special session in May 1797 and asked for accelerated construction of a navy. After the Revolution, Congress had let the navy lapse—fitful efforts at arming private merchantmen were all that were allowed, and then under strict orders to engage only French, Spanish, English, and Barbary Coast men-of-war. The time had come not only for a new navy but also for rejuvenated regular and militia forces.

Sadly enough, some of Adams's defense requests had been made before and had been generally ignored. George Washington's late 1780s lament for a navy to protect merchantmen did spur Congress to authorize building six frigates, but construction dragged on so long that in 1798 Congress replied to Adams's special message by urging that three of the vessels be swiftly finished and deployed. At that time the president was allowed to obtain, one way or another, twelve more war vessels and to commission in arms more than 350 American carriers. At last the frigates sailed and did serious damage to an unsuspecting French navy.

Persistently pushing diplomatic solutions to French problems, President Adams and his secretary of state, John Marshall, negotiated the Convention of 1800 (the Treaty of Mortefontaine) late that year. With the quasi naval war ended, both nations won most favored nation status. France promised return of American ships and crews and agreed to broad freedoms of commerce on the high seas and in mutual ports.

Elected president in 1800, Thomas Jefferson welcomed the Convention even as he inherited a festering mess with pirates on the northern coast of Africa. Since 1784 American ships had been victims of corsairs from Algiers, Morocco, Tripoli, and Tunis. Americans were late victims of the Barbary pirates. Preying on all Christian shipping for centuries, the pirates enslaved crews and passengers, and confiscated ships—all releasable for high ransom. Washington himself inveighed against the buccaneers—as, following world precedent, Congress appropriated ransom money in 1784 and Adams and Jefferson began negotiations. But in a decade Algiers captured eleven American ships and over a hundred prisoners. Congress upped the ransom to include providing a frigate and an annual donation of naval stores. By 1799 the Barbary pirates were temporarily pacified with money.

Angry American reaction sparked an 1800 slogan: "Millions for defense, but not one cent for tribute!" One Yankee envoy suggested that "there is but one language which can be held to these people, and this is *terror*." And when Tripoli declared war on the United States, President Jefferson—well supported by Congress—sent a naval squadron to patrol the North African coast and bombard Tripoli. Barbary campaigns by such early American naval heroes as Edward Preble, Stephen Decatur, and John Rodgers earned a shaky kind of stalemate.

Nothing seemed to calm the seas, especially as the Napoleonic wars engulfed much of Europe. A British blockade of French ports strained the Royal Navy, which began kidnapping crewmen from neutral vessels—they were claimed as strayed Englishmen—and again American ships suffered most. Both the blockade and impressment (kidnapping) of American crews nearly convinced Jefferson that his pro-French prejudices were sound. But when Napoleon proclaimed a counter-blockade, a cynical Jefferson sought ways to punish both offenders. Pushing an embargo of British and French trade, the president sought to protect American ships and seamen.

Jefferson blundered badly though boldly. The embargo barely ruffled European commerce but nearly wrecked America's economy—especially in the New England states, which lived on mercantilism. Dismal reports of decay there came steadily to the president. Dozens of ships languished in dock, their crews unpaid, their rigging rotting, their owners driven to smuggling and other ways of defying the law. Worst of all, Britain kept on impressing seamen while Napoleon ignored the president's gesture. Ruefully, Jefferson accepted repeal of the embargo late in his administration.

Elected America's chief executive in 1808, James Madison, who had been Jefferson's secretary of state, clutched his belief in American economic power as the best defense against foreign harassment. But he wobbled from one policy to another as New England resentment nearly reached rebellion; his drive for peace with honor resulted in neither.

2

•

Mr. Madison's War

James Madison's talents generally dwarfed his defects. High intellect, a suave pen, political vision, and a warm personality marked his genius. As his second presidential term began in 1813, he trusted experience to guide him through the increasingly roiling waters of international trade. Experience, though, did not serve him well, and a rising specter of war dimmed his hopes for peace. Politics also narrowed his options.

Chill winds of change ushered in a new Congress in 1811. From the elections of 1810 came a young group of southern and western "War Hawks" who fulminated about impressment, Indian agitation, and other insults by Albion; they damned Jefferson's and Madison's failed diplomacy and demanded war against Britain. Westerner Henry Clay became Speaker of the House of Representatives, Peter Porter chaired the House Committee on Foreign Affairs, and southerner Langdon Cheves took charge of the Ways and Means Committee. Famed South Carolina orator John C. Calhoun added orotundity to their attack on a "putrescent and ignominious peace."

At first things seemed to be going Madison's way. Most congressmen opposed war, but as the argument rose late in 1811 and continued into mid-1812 a subtle mind shift began. Madison himself, trying to fend off the War Hawks, clinging to a peace he had helped corrupt, offered to open

James Madison, Jefferson's secretary of state, fourth president (1809–1817). Courtesy of the Library of Congress.

trade to either Britain or Napoleon, depending on which accepted. It seemed a strategic moment to entice England while that nation was in the depths of trouble with Napoleon. The British government ignored what appeared a desperate plea from an inconsequential nation.

Even dovish congressmen grudgingly supported increased military funding and an expanded militia as a lever against Albion. That hope soon dashed, the War Hawks won a close House majority supporting a "second struggle for liberty." Enraged debates in the Senate reflected serious national uncertainty about war—especially in the trade-dependent northeastern states.

Newspapers, broadsides and rostrums, even pulpits, took sides. The following comment appeared in the New York *Evening Post* on January 24, 1812: "The wages proposed . . . to induce men to come forward and enlist for five years, leave their homes and march away to take Canada, is a bounty of $16, and $5 a month, with an uncharted section of wild land at the end." Since good men could make $15 a month from May to November "let the public judge if such inducements . . . will ever raise an army of 25,000 men, or ever were seriously expected to do it? . . . This may be called humbugging on a large scale."

An article titled "They Call It a War for Commerce?" in the *Evening Post* of January 26 put the issue financially. American exports in 1811, the writer noted, earned about $45 million, of which some $38 million came from England. "Let me ask you what you think of making war upon Great Britain and her allies, for the purpose of benefiting commerce?"

French flirtation with negotiations while England still strangled Yankee commerce made Britain the natural enemy. "War Should Be Declared" announced an editorial in the *Washington National Intelligencer* on April 14, 1811, despite wide claims of unpreparedness. "Our preparations are adequate to every essential object," urged the writer. After all, England's preoccupation with the Peninsular campaign, as well as with Sicily, India, and Ireland, foreclosed any chance of British troops coming to America. The British Navy went unmentioned.

A commentator in the New York *Evening Post* of April 21, 1812, harangued disgruntled northeasterners about the horrors of a likely war. "The expense will be enormous. It will ruin our country. . . . The desire to annex Canada to the United States is as base an ambition as ever burned in the bosom of Alexander." As for the Royal Navy, it would probably blockade the American coast from Maine to New Orleans. "The conflict will be long and severe . . . the final result doubtful. A nation that can debar the . . . conqueror of Europe from the sea, and resist his armies in Spain, will not surrender its provinces without a struggle." "Thousands of lives, millions of money, the flames of cities, the tears of widows and orphans" would be America's wages of war.

Ethnic threats were not forgotten in toting up the possibilities. An editorial titled "WAR!" in the *Columbian Centinel* of May 20, 1812, declared the British invulnerable and the conquest of Canada profitless and dangerous. "Our red brethren forgetful of the patriotic 'talks' of their 'father' Jefferson would pour down upon our frontier, and our black brethren" would opt for freedom in an endless conflict. "It is no longer doubtful that the Eastern States, are invincibly opposed to war."

A fiery editorial in *Niles Weekly Register* of May 30, 1812, reeked of offended patriotism and put the pro-war case in nearly irresistible terms. Hewing hard to a bedrock certainty that "the American people will never wage offensive war," the writer recites Britain's perfidies, including "the most flagrant violations of the individual, national and territorial rights of the American people." "We have suffered injuries, particularly in the wealth of our citizens, which no independent nation ever submitted to. Embargo was tried . . . and failed of its foreign operation. . . . We are driven into a corner, and must surrender at the discretion of a wicked and unprincipled enemy, or hew our way out of it—the hazard of life itself is preferable to the certain loss of all that makes it desirable."

Boldness would bring victory. Canada's certain capture would deny naval stores to Britain, undercut its commerce, weaken its hold on the West Indies, hurt its pride. Men and money would flood the ranks and treasury in a war to confirm American power.

Driven by disillusion with diplomacy, Madison reluctantly accepted the need for military preparations. More or less secret plans were made for a triple invasion of Canada if war came.

A kind of semi-war flickered in the northwest and the Great Lakes area, with Americans burning Toronto in April 1812, and when the USS *Constitution* bested HMS *Guerriere*, America swashed in martial pride.

Having once said that "the Ex[ecutive] is the branch of power most interested in war, & most prone to it," mindful that the Constitution, "with studied care, vested the question of war in the Legisl[ative]," Madison scrupulously left war making to Congress.[1] Accepting war as unavoidable, a saddened but determined president sent both houses a closely crafted message on June 1, 1812, recounting Britain's depredations, including inciting Indian atrocities, and noting America's efforts to keep the peace. The message laid out reasons but did not directly ask for war.

A divided Congress understood clearly enough, and a few days later the House voted 79-49 for war; opposition came mostly from the northeastern area. More deliberate, the Senate wrangled for days and voted once to a deadlock. But finally War Hawk rhetoric carried a 19-13 vote to pass "An Act Declaring War Between the United Kingdom of Great Britain and Ireland and the Dependencies Thereof and the United States of America and Their Territories." What many called "Mr. Madison's War" began when he signed the act on June 18, 1812, in hopes of quick success.

Despite earlier successes and loud war calls, Madison faced some cold realities. America could expect delayed resources—regular army recruiting would expand, militias would straggle to the call; most people might pay higher taxes. Much time and treasure would be wasted, though, while America mobilized. Clamor for action did force a sober president to push the three planned Canadian invasions. They failed in a weltering of blood, ill luck, and panic.

Most early ground fighting went to the British, while a largely new American navy won unexpected battles at sea. Some sparks of hope touched the somber skies of 1812 with the news that the USS *Constitution* had bested not only HMS *Guerriere* but also HMS *Java* in actions where shots bounced off the *Constitution* and won her the nickname *Old Iron-sides*. Other Yankee ships scored glittering successes on the high seas.

Still, menacing enemy forces gathered along the northern rim of war. An Indian-British army moved toward Indiana, while a strong fleet cruised to control the Great Lakes, retake Indian lands, and pierce America's heartland.

Two sudden and unexpected victories solidified the northwestern frontier. On September 10, 1813, young Oliver Hazard Perry, with a small fleet he had bought and built along the Great Lakes, wrecked an enemy flotilla at the Battle of Put-in-Bay on Lake Erie. His terse report to Gen. William Henry Harrison: "We have met the enemy and they are ours." Within a month, Harrison, commanding in the northwest, attacked a combined British-Indian force in the Battle of the Thames; the British decamped while the Indians fought on until the death of their great chief Tecumseh broke their spirit and their power.

British strategy in the American War wobbled from attempted attacks to sober defensives and rather aimless use of the Royal Navy. Some superannuated generals led wretchedly and wasted both lives and opportunities; some hewed to the best Redcoat tradition. Various blockades were tried but often leaked and allowed deadly Yankee cruisers abroad. Through most of 1813 both sides fought a disjointed, somewhat haphazard war. Britain still fought Napoleon, and the United States fought to mobilize and find a coherent strategy.

When Napoleon surrendered in March 1814, London concentrated on America. Britain reinforced its Canadian ranks and deployed forces in a three-pronged drive of its own—at Chesapeake Bay, on Lake Champlain, and at the mouth of the Mississippi. They blockaded large areas of American coasts, and captured and burned the White House and the Capitol in August (Madison saw it all as his war came home to roost). Baltimore and Fort McHenry held them off in September 1814—a triumph that inspired lawyer Francis Scott Key's poem, "The Star-Spangled Banner." Although the war was slowly going its way, Britain offered to talk peace. Serious negotiations started in Ghent, but dragged on as the sides traded victories.

Finally the pesky and expensive little American conflict led to an October 1814 British offer of peace on the basis of both sides keeping what they had won. Talk continued. More American successes, especially the repulse of a large force advancing at Lake Champlain and Gen. Andrew Jackson's thrashing of the Creek Indians in the south, changed the tone at Ghent.

There were disheartening moments for Madison. On December 15, 1814, a gathering of angry and commercially threatened New Englanders

Gen. Andrew Jackson. "Old Hickory," the Hero of New Orleans, 1815. Seventh president (1829–1837). Copy of lithograph by James Baillie. Courtesy of the Library of Congress.

met in convention at Hartford, Connecticut. This nearly rebellious gathering to push protection of New England's trading interests, to propose constitutional amendments protecting states' rights, even secession, and to restrict Madison's obvious military bent, sloughed into frustration as the war ended. American persistence, aptly aided by slow communication to England, dimmed British enthusiasm for a war running on beyond patience. The Treaty of Ghent, signed in December 1814, ended the war as it started—*status quo ante bellum*. By the time Congress ratified the treaty in February 1815, General Jackson's smashing victory in the Battle of New Orleans confirmed America's success.

Madison's friend, the French minister, put the war in international perspective: "[T]hree years of warfare have been a trial of the capacity of [American] institutions to sustain a state of war, a question . . . now resolved in their advantage. Finally the war has given the Americans what they substantially lacked, a national character founded on a glory common to all." Mr. Madison's War preserved Congress's war power and annealed his nation.

Evolution of an Army

Important lessons were offered from the War of 1812—not all of them salutary. Most flaws were ignored in victory. Certainly the United States Navy needed expanding since it sustained hope of winning while the enemy won on land. Moreover, the navy made American repute as a power in the world. Still, regulars and militia certainly proved themselves at Baltimore, Chippewa, Lundy's Lane, and Horseshoe Bend, and at Jackson's astounding New Orleans win in January 1815. Americans rejoiced that their variegated forces had stopped the British once again.

Grumblers, though—they always crop up as spoilers—argued that America's ramshackle military organization had barely held together. Field experience patched over bad organization, terrible supply gaps, balking leadership, wretched training—and now victory seemed certain to excuse everything. Clearly, some argued, the regulars at Chippewa and Lundy's Lane did prove the value of training and show the danger

James Monroe, secretary of state (1811–1814), concurrently secretary of state and of war (September 1814–March 1815), secretary of state (1815–1817), and fifth president (1817–1825). Author of Monroe Doctrine. Painting by Robert Walter Weir. Courtesy of the Library of Congress.

of relying on militia. Equal truculence came from those who argued that the Minute Man tradition lingered as the militia did well in many places, especially in the South under Andrew Jackson's steady hand. A national consensus quickly embraced the notion that the country could defend itself—even the hemisphere—with a smaller military establishment. Washington's support of a professional army was not forgotten.

President Madison and his successor, James Monroe (who had served for a time as secretary of war and, in 1823, proclaimed the Monroe Doctrine excluding foreign intervention in the Americas), saw weaknesses clearly enough and knew that national security demanded military improvements.

John C. Calhoun ranks as the biggest improvement; he became secretary of war in Monroe's administration. A born organizer, he wrestled the War Department into modern times. He trusted graduates of the relatively new United States Military Academy—a school out of fashion in the egalitarian dawn of the nineteenth century— and distributed them carefully around the army after he had made a careful study of his new domain. Seizing on wartime innovations in bringing such staff functions as ordnance, engineering, and supply into the capital, Calhoun created professional bureaus that lasted most of the century. Pushing several army reorganizations, he created an ambiguous office of general in chief, which begged the question of who really commanded the army and provided an agitation platform for its longest incumbent, Winfield Scott (1841–1861). Calhoun also supervised a new divisional structure, emphasized practical guns and tactics for the artillery, and rationalized fi-

John C. Calhoun, secretary of war (1817–1825) under President Monroe and vice president (1825–1832) under Presidents J. Q. Adams and Jackson. Courtesy of the Library of Congress.

nances. Foreign ideas and weapons won his attention; American officers went abroad to return with fresh manuals, designs, and thoughts.

Joel R. Poinsett, a Calhoun successor in the late 1830s and early 1840s, had his own energy and vision. He equipped and supported light artillery batteries and welcomed major changes in infantry weapons. Muskets fired by fulminate of mercury percussion caps—which made them serviceable in bad weather—replaced flintlocks as classic smoothbores yielded to longer ranged, much more accurate rifles. Cartridges with paper-wrapped powder attached made loading faster and easier.

A nearly new navy appeared after the War of 1812. The Navy Department gave independence and momentum to new, larger warships, innovative strategy, and advances in ordnance; shipwrighting advanced from slow art to quicker science. America's corsairs protected commerce, and their boldness bolstered international admiration from the Dead Sea to the Pacific and the Sea of Japan. Following army experience to some extent, navy staff bureaus appeared at Washington in 1842, and, as the navy copied the army, a naval academy opened at Annapolis in 1845.

All these advances showed a vast change in command and control. Professional officers slowly replaced the old-line amateurs lingering from earlier wars. Best of all, American presidents took deeper interest in martial matters and exercised closer executive oversight over the secretaries as America's military structure became coherent, manageable, and flexible. Certainly more improvements were needed, but the United States approached war with its Mexican neighbor far better prepared than ever before.

3

•

The War with Mexico

Wild and woolly happenings brought the United States and Mexico to angry confrontation in 1845. After nine years of independence blurred by Mexican and Indian hostility, economic fragility, and internal fussing, the tough little Republic of Texas finally agreed to join the Union. Quickly Texas leaders knew that they were not entirely welcome as the twenty-eighth state of the Union. Squabbling centered in the North, where fears of more power to the slave-holding South troubled politics.

Fortunately for Texas, a fervently expansionist U.S. president, James K. Polk, followed through on a platform promise to annex the Republic and signed enabling legislation in December 1845. Instantly Mexicans erupted; they had never really accepted the Republic and saw the United States as stealing part of their country.

A determined Polk grabbed for more land in disputed areas of Oregon Territory—hence the political slogan "54-40 or Fight"—and also wanted California's Pacific ports. His blunt diplomacy, American terms or war, inflamed many but cowed more.

He expected trouble, since Mexico would be the big loser in his scheme: Texas, plus all the land from Santa Fe westward, constituted about half of the country. He offered $20 million and assumption of all American claims for California and New Mexico, and war was the bruited alternative.

Polk threatened war but dallied with peace through a mercurial, possibly brilliant Mexican politician-turncoat-soldier, Antonio López de Santa Anna, whose controversial role during the Texas Revolution had made him an exile. Dangling a negotiated partition of his country, he went through the U.S. blockade. As soon as he was home, he rallied troops against the invaders!

Neither disillusioned nor surprised, Polk sent Gen. Zachary Taylor and an efficient American force into the disputed lands of South Texas. This brought the war Polk anticipated, a war that he not only goaded but one he would command with widely expanding executive power. Polk, in fact, became the first president really to function as the commander-in-chief. With a pliable, if not weak, secretary of war in William Marcy, the president propounded not only strategy but also tactics, often kicked a lazy logistical system, feuded with his Whig generals Winfield Scott and Zachary Taylor, used the navy adroitly in California waters, and consolidated civilian control of war.

Strategically innovative, Polk devised a "cordon" offensive—several attacks launched simultaneously—which fragmented resistance. As Taylor's victorious army fought its way from South Texas into northern Mexico from May to September 1846, Polk sent another expedition from Ft. Leav-

James K. Polk, eleventh president (1845–1849). Polk's prosecution of the Mexican War resulted in U.S. acquisition of California and territory in the Southwest. Copy of engraving c. 1840s by H. W. Smith. Courtesy of the Library of Congress.

enworth, Kansas, that took a defenseless Santa Fe and went on to a warm welcome in California, where the U.S. Navy had already captured important coastal towns. Another U.S. column struck isolated El Paso del Norte as Mexico's forces lost every battle of the new war.

Despite the irritatingly Whiggish presidential ambitions of his two highest commanders (Taylor would succeed in his), Democrat Polk stuck with them. The generals, in turn, became jealous of each other and paranoid about Polk. Somehow, though, all three conjured an alliance of mutual distrust that sustained them to victory.

Though some historians argue that Polk's war with Mexico is simply another example of Leviathan smashing a midget, Mexico fought hard. Santa Fe and California were too far away to save, but Santa Anna, who had gathered a host of 25,000 and knew that Gen. Winfield Scott's army was getting many of Taylor's men, met "Old Rough and Ready" on February 22, 1847, at Buena Vista, near Saltillo, Mexico. Heavily outnumbered, Taylor won the day because of superior artillery and won the second day because of a fierce attack by Col. Jefferson Davis and his Mississippi volunteers. Surrounded by his own dead and wounded (some 40 percent of his army), Santa Anna began a searing 400-mile retreat to Mexico City. Undaunted, he took money from the Catholic Church, used conscription, and built another army to meet Yankees coming west along the road from Vera Cruz, where Scott's successful amphibious landing set new precedents in expeditionary warfare.

Scott's campaign also set precedents in daring and innovation. Heading inland from Vera Cruz on April 8, 1847, with about 12,000 men, Scott's troops fought varied skirmishes and won a major battle at Cerro Gordo on April 12—young West Pointers were key factors—but were halted by yellow fever and the departure of short-enlistment men. With reduced ranks, Scott decided to abandon his communications and live off the country. Against Santa Anna's recruited 25,000, Scott led his 10,000 to a series of major, bitterly contested battles around Mexico City that won the capital and ended the war in Mexico's surrender—confirmed by the Treaty of Guadalupe Hildalgo in February 1848.

Whether driven by hubris or vainglory, Polk had reason to gloat. His bold diplomacy had firmed the United States' northern border and established the southern frontier of Texas, while acquiring much of New Mexico, Arizona, California, and territories that became Colorado, Nevada, and Utah.

Military lessons abounded. Deeds of such West Pointers as Pierre G. T. Beauregard, Robert E. Lee, and George B. McClellan confirmed the need

Gen. Winfield Scott. "Old Fuss and Feathers" served in the War of 1812 and the Mexican War, and was first U.S. General-in-Chief, a position he held from the outset of the Civil War until his retirement in November 1861 at age seventy-five. Courtesy of the Library of Congress.

for professionals at arms. Taylor's and Scott's battles, plus the work of an unknown Lt. T. J. Jackson's guns in several actions, proved the ascendancy of artillery on the battlefield. Scott's use of secret funds enhanced the importance of spying, and his kind relations with Mexican civilians taught important lessons in logistical self-sufficiency and military government.

First and foremost, Polk had virtually commanded the war and established the martial power of the chief executive.

Dangers Old and New

Success with Mexico could be rightly touted, yet an old enigma lingered to muffle boasts of "Manifest Destiny." Years of confrontation, years of conciliation, years of butchery tangled Anglo-Indian relations into a remorseless tragedy. From early days at Jamestown, Indians tried to stop the flood of white invasion with everything from friendship to deception, terror, torture, hostile alliances, and war. In the end, nothing worked, and tribal lands shrank against the spreading stain of conquest.

Tecumseh's defeat at the Thames in 1813 muffled Indian problems until the Black Hawk War in 1832—an attempt by Sauk leader Black Hawk to move 2,000 of his people across the Mississippi into Illinois. U.S. militia and regulars went against him. This melancholy affair ended with a ruinous militia attack that drove exhausted Sauk survivors to final defeat and to a reservation. As a result, other midwestern tribes also left their homelands and moved west.

In the South various Creek tribes coalesced to stem the flood of white encroachment. Their gathered forces were nearly annihilated in Alabama by Gen. Andrew Jackson at the Battle of Horseshoe Bend in March 1814. Sporadic Cherokee resistance eroded, and in the late 1830s remnants were pushed westward on the shameful Trail of Tears. Florida's hardy Seminoles waged a series of wars against the whites in the 1830s, 1840s, and 1850s. Some hung on in the swamps and glades; most, though, were rounded up and moved to reservations somewhere in the dry, inhospitable West.

"Reservation" is a noun with varied definitions, two of which applied aptly to the American Indians: "the act of keeping back, withholding, or setting apart"; "the act of making an exception or qualification." These places of segregation and deprivation grew increasingly in what would become Oklahoma—supposedly far enough from white settlement to solve the Indian problem. So it seemed at the end of the Mexican War.

Continuing settlement, though, confounded the Indian solution. In 1848 an engulfing human tsunami flooded California. Gold! Where the yellow ore beckoned came good men and bad, artisans, engineers, sailors, rich and poor, harlots and wives in a wash of humanity that banished all conventions in a terrible greed for ground. The immediate victims were the fragmented local Indian tribes—they were pushed aside or slaughtered in various wars. As one historian said, "[I]f Euro-Americans committed genocide anywhere on the continent against Native Americans, it was in California," where their numbers dwindled from 150,000 in 1850 to 35,000 in a decade.[1] Deep running hatreds bubbled from the Indian conflicts, keeping wounds open and hostility rampant.

From the Mexican War, Americans remembered President Polk's commanding leadership (which sometimes snarled the command structure) as well as the costs of success. Victory for the United States came not so much from generalship (Scott showed real professionalism) but from careful training, quick studies by citizen soldiers, and the gifted work of the young West Point graduates. It came, too, from sound logistics, effective artillery, and an uncommon willingness to learn from mistakes. Predictably, postwar stagnation fogged memories, and many good things learned were forgotten.

Stagnation revived parochialism. Presidents increasingly ignored the military, and several sought to reduce its size and costs. Incompetent secretaries of war lost control of their department. Navy secretaries were marginally better, but their brief ran shorter with retrenchment. The Commanding General of the Army filled a poorly defined job with uncertain authority. The various supply and technical bureau chiefs created personal fiefdoms without concern for each other's duties or for national military needs, and rarely recognized superiors. When the Civil War erupted, the U.S. Army lacked visibility, money, size, and self-confidence, while the U.S. Navy boasted barely forty ships in commission.

One of the great debates in American historiography centers on what caused the Civil War. Some argue for slavery as the first cause; others for the different ways North and South regarded the Constitution and the Union, or for a cultural chasm between neo-industrialism and agriculture; still others for southern nationalism or the antislavery movement. There is truth to all of these arguments, but they are spawn of a break in American ideology, a cosmic change in the way freedom was defined. In the North freedom was enshrined in independence as the bulwark of the nation; freedom came to personal dimensions with Jefferson's triumph in 1800 and the rise of reform sentiment. Southerners saw freedom in political and economic terms, as liberty strictly defined in a constitution that protected the states, which, in turn, protected their citizens.

Simply stated, northerners thought of the Union as it, southerners as we. Jefferson and Madison caught the difference in the Virginia and Kentucky Resolutions of the 1790s and staked a case for state sovereignty. Although federal power increased through the strains and challenges of the nineteenth century, the notion of the Union as a confederation never died.

Strengths and weaknesses of the nation were tested by the Missouri Compromise in 1820, which supposedly prohibited slavery in new territory above 36°30' north latitude; by South Carolina's discriminatory tariff-inspired attempt at nullification in the late 1830s; and by the Compromise of 1850, which once again tried to bridge the fault of slavery's extension into new states and territories. Harriet Beecher Stowe's 1852 novel, *Uncle Tom's Cabin*, with its scenes of vicious cruelties to slaves, of loving Uncle Tom beaten to death, churned a deep-running current of reform in northern psyches to foaming outrage. It seemed to prove all bad things said of the South, to justify resistance. Certainly it helped passage of state legislation aimed at nullifying the tough Fugitive Slave Act enacted as part of the 1850 Compromise. The Compromise, though, worked fairly well until the admission of Kansas and Nebraska as new territories again rocked the Union.

The southern political struggle to keep senatorial parity between slave and free lands suffered under the Missouri Compromise. In 1854 Senator Stephen A. Douglas of Illinois proposed what he called "popular sovereignty" in organizing the huge territorial areas of Kansas and Nebraska: settlers could decide the issue of slave or free lands. Congress, by adopting Douglas's scheme, brushed aside the Missouri Compromise and opened all potential territories to slavery—a position apparently confirmed when in 1857 the Supreme Court handed down its famed Dred Scott decision, which pronounced the Missouri Compromise line unconstitutional. Soon bitter fighting between free-soil men and slaveholders produced the cauldron of "Bleeding Kansas," a cauldron fermented by zealot John Brown's antislavery slaughters. By no means all northerners were antislavery: a good deal of racism tinged Yankee feelings. Political opinion swayed and old issues faded. Weak President James Buchanan, elected in 1856, failed to solve anything or smooth issues as the 1860 national election loomed.

For southerners, slavery's extension had moral, economic, and constitutional importance. Extension would ensure the plantation system's future amid fresh land and commerce; it would broaden slavery's base and support its morality. For southerners, the most important of all considerations was the right of property: if slaves could be taken away, so could other kinds of personal possessions.

Rhetoric and reason shifted in the tumultuous 1850s, and by the end of the decade so had patriotism. Bitterness about the extension of slavery grew, finally, to bitterness about different ways of life as minds closed and meanings changed. In the North antislavery rhetoric from varied pulpits expanded exponentially until evangelical prejudice passed for logic. Friendships broke, churches sundered, professional groups divided, laws were used against laws as northern states passed personal liberty statutes freeing all slaves within their borders. Editorial writers turned against slavery and its defenders. Old standard magazines followed suit and stirred controversy by excluding much southern material. Added to rising antislavery sentiment was weariness with endless bleating about "southern rights" and secession threats. Not a few northerners came to think of "letting the erring sisters go in peace" and be rid of the whole mess. The hanging of terrorist John Brown in Charles Town, Virginia, in December 1859 made abolitionists of many moderates; Ralph Waldo

Emerson pronounced that martyred zealot a saint to "make the gallows glorious like the cross."

Southerners came slowly to a kind of garrison attitude as they felt the venom spilling on them and the Constitution's protection of slavery obviously thinned. Planters especially felt threatened since they got blamed for whatever sins the South committed. No matter that there were few enough of them and not many owned many slaves, guilt stuck to them like tar. And they were the leaders of fashion in a South they hoped could remain slower, less frenetic, and more human than the industrializing North. Leaders of politics, too, they came to fear the future and finally turned against it. Not all of them, by any means, wanted separation; they were, after all, agricultural entrepreneurs who depended on northern money to survive. Most southerners, though, wasted little concern on the rising controversy. Mainly farmers and artisans, scattered bankers, cotton factors, and other small urban types—and, of course, politicians—they were finally alarmed by the fire-eating editorials, the chants of Yankee perfidy coming from their pulpits, their newspapers, their elected officials. At last they shared the garrison mind-set and waited for the election of 1860 with a kind of wistful dread.

American national elections had traditionally sported debates, raucous stump speaking, exotic entertainments, and hard cider. There were speeches aplenty in 1860, but few debates as ideas became dogma; fireworks and snake-dances lost their innocence and became propaganda theater; liquor saluted shifting patriotism. Everyone knew that the coming election would be a referendum on the Union.

Everyone knew, too, something of the new cast of characters dominating the American future. "The Little Giant," Stephen A. Douglas, kept prominence as he still pursued the Democratic nomination—he would have been a shoo-in save for his famous debates with Illinoisan Abraham Lincoln in 1858. Lincoln, an attorney of some local renown, claimed national note as he persistently hoisted Douglas on his own petard of popular sovereignty. As Douglas wriggled, southerners scrambled away and his party fragmented. The new Republican Party—an agglomeration of several free-soil and free-labor groups—gave its standard to Lincoln and hoped he could charm more than abolitionists. By adroit rhetoric, he did.

In the swash of the Democratic convention in Charleston, South Carolina, the party buckled. Douglas supporters were stunned when Alabama fire-eater William Lowndes Yancey presented the Alabama Platform, a set of demands that held the Union hostage: protection of slavery in the territories, strict enforcement of the Fugitive Slave Act of 1850, plus a constitutional guarantee of southern minority rights. The demands were perennials; the way they were presented made a tragic difference. When the convention could not argue itself to total acceptance, delegates from seven states walked out with Yancey. A Southern Democratic Party soon formed, as did a Constitutional Union Party, and the fragmentation gave the Republicans much advantage.

Lincoln won. Although a minority president in popular voting, he won 180 electoral votes to 123 for three arrayed against him.

"Black Republican" Lincoln's success ignited secession. This national sundering also fragmented the U.S. Army. For a time officers' oaths bound them to the Union, but animosities weakened devotions and sparked suspicion. Louisianian Pierre G. T. Beauregard became superintendent of the military academy at West Point in January 1861, but was quickly replaced because of his southern background. Virginian Winfield Scott, Commanding General of the Army, stayed with the Union while a prominent colleague and fellow Virginian, Robert E. Lee, wrestled with his conscience and finally joined the Confederacy. So, at last, most of the officer corps divided: southern ranks would bask in talent.

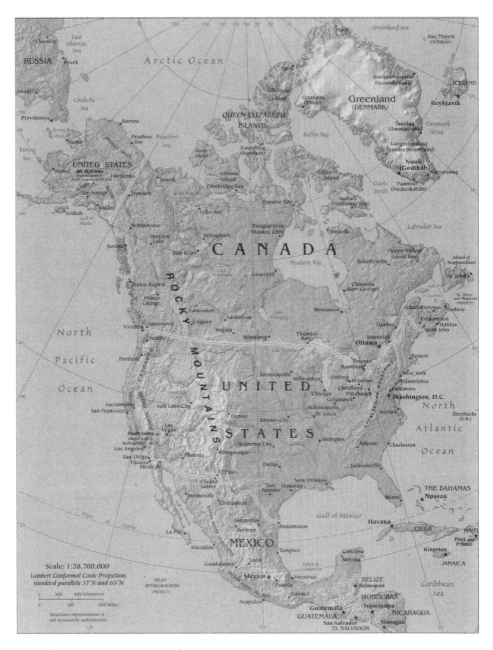

Map of North America. Courtesy of Texas A&M University Depository.

4

•

The Civil War

For President-Elect Lincoln, the future came too soon. During the months between his election and inauguration, his country fragmented and his challenges exploded. For a brief time he nursed the idea that the crisis was exaggerated and might subside; secession of seven slave states by the end of February 1861 banished that hope.

As a kind of chaotic inertia dulled the North, the South formed a new government in Montgomery, Alabama, installed Jefferson Davis, eminent statesman from Mississippi, as the president, and began arming for war. Southern moderates were swamped by raucous calls for a new country as a different dream appeared.

In those apprentice months, a frustrated Lincoln heard of the struggling "Peace Convention" droning ineffectually in the capital, of a proposed "unamenable amendment" to guarantee slavery once again, and he groped toward ways to save the Union. He believed secession unconstitutional, as had Buchanan, but, unlike that baffled executive, felt he had to stop it somehow. He knew that slavery complicated the emergency and that his opposition to extending slavery beyond its natural limits not only frightened southerners but also chilled many of his northern friends. Still, further truckling, he guessed, would only postpone trouble, and he urged congressional friends to stand firm. "The tug has to come," he wrote, "&

better now, than any time hereafter."[1] He tried to juggle some lingering uncertainty by focusing on the Union, not race, as the divisive problem. A Republican administration, he protested, would not attack slavery, would, in fact, protect it; expansion, though, would be resisted.

Meanwhile he watched Montgomery and read what Davis and his southern government did and said. The Confederates were cautious about most problems but serious about their new Confederacy; secession had come to stay. Making several important speeches on his way to his own inauguration, Lincoln talked of a country dimly seen, a country growing beyond itself as an engine of liberty for the world as he felt the force of history.

History loomed over him like a colossus, and he caught something of it in his farewell remarks at Springfield, Illinois, in February 1861: "I now leave . . . with a task before me greater than that which rested upon Washington."

Hardly true, that idea is nearly bronzed in Lincoln's myth. Different tasks they faced, Washington to lead a fragile revolution against a great power and make a nation from colonies, Lincoln to suppress a rebellion and keep that nation whole. If Lincoln's task seems lesser now, he nonetheless pursued it with Washington's devotion.

Lincoln reached Washington for inaugural ceremonies as a virtual unknown, and when he rose to speak on March 4, 1861, he looked an unlikely leader at a crossroads of history. Lincoln's address rewards careful study. In this one speech, he proclaimed a policy of preserving the Union, focused on slavery as the issue in dispute, fixed any war guilt on the South, and put America's crisis in terms of political reason—not bad for a presidential neophyte.

Confederate relations consumed much of the new president's time. Adroitly refusing to meet with commissioners from Jefferson Davis, he left them to the tender mercies of his secretary of state, redoubtable William H. Seward. Seward played them with seasoned diplomatic deceit as they talked about disposing of public property, especially Fort Sumter in Charleston harbor. For the Confederates, Fort Sumter signified sovereignty; for Lincoln, it symbolized his promise to protect public property.

Wrangling soon convinced the Confederate emissaries of Seward's perfidy, and they went back south. President Davis and his cabinet argued the next step and decided Fort Sumter had to be taken to validate the Confederacy. Early on April 12, 1861, Rebel guns—commanded by Davis's new brigadier general, P.G.T. Beauregard—opened fire on Sumter.

Lincoln grabbed the moment and in two days called for 75,000 volunteers to put down insurrection. Going to Congress for a war declaration

Abraham Lincoln. This photograph was taken April 9, 1865, the day Gen. Robert E. Lee surrendered at Appomattox. President Lincoln would be assassinated at Ford's Theatre on April 14, 1865. Courtesy of the Library of Congress.

was unnecessary and ruinous since it would recognize the existence of the Confederate States. Lawyer Lincoln realized that a massive rebellion taxed definitions of insurrection. There would be outcries as he broadened executive authority to make war, but if Congress supported him, he would push for a quick end to southern pretensions. Congress's tacit support came in funding the call for volunteers.

Deeply concerned about having to suspend the right of habeas corpus and curtail freedom of speech, Lincoln offered an elaborately convoluted explanation to Congress on July 4, 1861. He saw it as a duty, he said, to permit the military "to arrest, and detain, without resort to the ordinary processes and forms of law, such individuals as might . . . [be] dangerous to the public safety." If, indeed, those detentions broke the law, he argued that the Confederates were breaking all the laws, and asked, "[A]re all the laws, *but one*, to go unexecuted, and the government itself to go to pieces, lest that one be violated?" Then came an interesting rationalization: "Even in such a case, would not the official oath be broken, if the government should be overthrown, when it was believed that disregarding the single law, would tend to preserve it?"

Lincoln created new powers as he fought a pragmatist's war. "Military necessity," like "national security" in later times, legitimized press censorship, arbitrary arrests for sedition (an estimated 20,000 people were detained), military suppression of labor strikes, and civil unrest.

Some historians argue that Lincoln's damping of dissent stifled democracy. Others suggest that the resulting fierce discussions of liberties expanded appreciation of the Constitution as a document flexible enough to sustain its own defense. Lincoln's warring above it seemed to confirm its utility. When, in September 1862, after a thin Union victory at Antietam, Maryland, he issued his Preliminary Emancipation Proclamation, Lincoln guessed he had probably gone too far. Freeing the slaves by waving a presidential edict smacked of dictatorship unrestrained. And he had not wanted to do it; his ideas were less radical. As he explained to Horace Greeley in August 1862: "My paramount object in this struggle *is* to save the Union, and is *not* either to save or to destroy slavery. If I could save the Union without freeing *any* slave I would do it; and if I could save it by freeing some and leaving others alone I would also do that."[2]

He recognized that the war had eroded northern morale and knew he had to revive a flagging North by something new, a new war aim that might make the Union's cause a new thrust of freedom. He thought his Emancipation Proclamation unconstitutional but relied on history's vindication.

Gen. Ulysses S. Grant, Commander-in-Chief of the Union Army, 1864–1865; eighteenth U.S. president (1869–1877). Other Civil War veterans who became president were Andrew Johnson, Rutherford B. Hayes, James A. Garfield, Chester A. Arthur, Benjamin Harrison, and William McKinley. Courtesy of National Archives.

So it went for him as he grew beyond his office to evoke the dim vision seen after the triumph at Gettysburg: there, in November 1863, Lincoln made a short speech—nearly lost in the shuffling following a lengthy oration ahead of him. The war, he said, tested whether a "nation conceived in liberty, and dedicated to the proposition that all men are created equal . . . can long endure. . . . From these honored dead we take increased devotion . . . we here highly resolve that these dead shall not have died in vain—that this nation, under God, shall have a new birth of freedom—and that government of the people, by the people, for the people, shall not perish from the earth."

Military necessities shadowed that new birth of freedom. Naval matters were competently handled by a gifted navy secretary, Gideon Welles. Army problems crowded beyond an incompetent war minister and forced Lincoln into direct army command. Short militia service hardly qualified the new commander-in-chief as a war leader, but legal and legislative experience taught some things about war management. Relying first on venerable Winfield Scott, 1812 veteran and long General of the Army, Lincoln found him fit for strategy but unfit for the field. His Anaconda Plan for dividing the Confederacy made sense, but younger generals would be needed to make it work. In a hectic search for competent commanders, Lincoln fixed first on Irwin McDowell to raise an army and invade Virginia. McDowell's good plans failed against the Rebel army in the First Battle of Bull Run, in July 1861. Lincoln turned with some trepidation to a Democrat, Gen. George B. McClellan, West Pointer turned railroad builder, dapper, vain, voluble, and vincible. When McClellan's swash buckled at Antietam, Lincoln increased his own war management. Still seeking commanders bold enough to use superior resources against weaker, he suggested strategy, even tactics, to a lengthy list of mediocrities: John Pope, Ambrose Burnside, Joseph Hooker in the east; Don Carlos Buell, Henry W. Halleck, John McClernand in the west. Offering large opportunities in department command to most of these men and watching them fail, Lincoln struggled on to manage military and civil affairs himself. He fixed at last on a rising western star, Gen. Ulysses S. Grant, whose victories at Shiloh and Vicksburg showed the things most missing in Union commanders—daring and relentless drive. When the president appointed Grant to command all Federal armies in early 1864, he found a man who could beat the great Rebel general Robert E. Lee—who had earlier been offered the Union command. Through all of Grant's campaigns, Lincoln urged, pushed, supplied, rallied, until at last he conjured victory.

Saving the Union surely justified any wartime measures, even sheathing the Constitution for a time. And yet what would emerge in a "new birth of

Gen. Robert E. Lee, Commander of the Army of Northern Virginia, C.S.A., 1862–1865. Courtesy of the Library of Congress.

freedom"? Lincoln had some qualms as the war became a remorseless smashing of old things and created a new nation of machines, money, and power enough to invent its own future. He tried to slow Leviathan but was shot down too soon. The people now worked for the state.

A good deal of the same kind of changing happened in the South. Jefferson Davis, a model states' rights man, faced more Washingtonian challenges than his northern counterpart. His the task of forging a nation out of sovereign states, awaking a new nationalism and sustaining it in the midst of war against an awakening colossus. He became first and last the foremost Confederate as he turned the Confederate constitution against the states and made them into a nation. The constitution legitimized a draft and supported his tough methods against sedition, treason, and fraud. "Military necessity" led him, also, to enlarge the constitution as he centralized the government to manage both society and the economy to achieve a different patriotism.

Like Lincoln, Davis became a strong American war president; and like Lincoln, he searched widely for aggressive commanders. He gambled and lost on Braxton Bragg and John Pemberton in western operations, on John Bell Hood and Joseph E. Johnston in eastern operations. At last he found Lee, who solved the eastern problem and nearly won the war.

Jefferson Davis, veteran of the Black Hawk War (1832) and the Mexican War (1846–1847), secretary of war (1853–1857), and president of the Confederacy (1861–1865). Courtesy of the Library of Congress.

Like Lincoln, too, Davis took direct charge of campaigning when generals failed their tests. He, too, suggested strategy and tactics, while supporting his armies to the full limits of southern resources. At the last, with his country unraveling around him, he urged emancipation and offered it for foreign recognition of the Confederacy. When the war ended and the myth began, the South had become a small, centralized, industrial nation led by a "strict constructionist" who had dredged the power of the constitution. Ineluctably, though, the Confederacy had become almost a mirror image of the enemy.

A hard question from the Civil War: What kind of democracy survived?

Last Days of the Old Army

Reconstruction cemented Union power as Congress asserted its authority and forced military occupation of the South and reformation of American politics. President Andrew Johnson, dimmed in Lincoln's shadow, lost control not only of Reconstruction's process but also of the army as it became involved in supporting, even sustaining, civil administrations.

Even so, ranks, ships, and budgets shrank in the postwar years as the nation surged into a new economy of industrialism sustained by a long peace. Businessmen, especially those involved in foreign trade, soon saw war as a fearsome enemy; hence the corollary notion that armies also were enemies. In the 1870s, 1880s and 1890s, many wartime generals dropped to their regular army ranks, while a good many American capitalists, despite devotion to Darwinian survival of the fittest notions, saw the cost of guns, troops, ships, and supplies simply as waste. Congress

President Andrew Johnson receiving some of his "dissatisfied fellow countrymen," delegates of various Sioux tribes, East Room, White House, February 23, 1867. Courtesy of the Library of Congress.

A Dash for Timber, Frederic Remington, 1889. The mounted Plains Indians were called the finest light cavalry in the world. Their subjugation taught the U.S. Army hard-won lessons in guerrilla warfare. Courtesy of the Library of Congress.

largely agreed—and in 1877 ignored army appropriations until the end of November. Officers borrowed money while the ranks survived on short rations. Irrelevance dogged America's military, and its numbers dwindled from about 50,000 to under 30,000 in the 1890s. No major conflicts frightened the country, and the draggling Indian campaigns became a commonplace. In 1890 the tragic fight at Wounded Knee ended the Indian wars. At that same time the Census Bureau proclaimed the closing of America's internal frontier. Suddenly those long years of scarce troopers riding against such tough foemen as Cochise, Geronimo, Satanta, and Chief Joseph ended along with the men, horses, log forts, and guns of the "Old Army."

There were breaks in boredom. Sending over 1,000 U.S. Marines into Panama in 1885, President Grover Cleveland stepped boldly into continental affairs. An emerging pattern saw U.S. troops increasingly stationed in Central America in the wake of wars and rebellions that threatened American interests. Panama slowly became a kind of Yankee protectorate.

In the doldrum years for the army, the United States Navy expanded. A Naval War College appeared in 1882 and soon produced such thinkers as Alfred Thayer Mahan, author of the classic *Influence of Sea Power upon History, 1660–1783* (1890). American Caribbean ventures focused attention on the navy. Cruisers were built and a battleship program began.

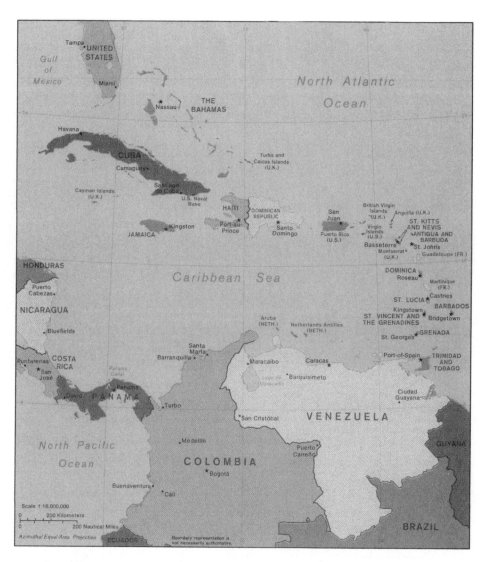

Map of Caribbean and Central America. Courtesy of Texas A&M University Depository.

5

•

The Spanish-American War

Then came the war with Spain that saw Congress take direct and unusual control in launching a conflict. Troubles had been bubbling since the *Virginius* affair in 1873, when Spain captured that vessel loaded with arms for the Cuban rebels and shot some fifty-four passengers and crew, including many Americans. President U.S. Grant nearly went to war. America's deep-running fancy for underdogs fueled trouble with Spain. For some time hard-pressed rebels fought for freedom from an increasingly tyrannical colonialism—and they were losing slowly. Stories of torture and of women and children dying in concentration camps not far from the United States sparked American concern.

President William McKinley's serious diplomatic efforts won some Spanish concessions while rebellion continued and Yankee support for the Cuban rebels reached near-crusade levels. War seemed imminent when the battleship USS *Maine* mysteriously exploded and sank in Havana harbor on February 15, 1898. Civil War veteran McKinley, who shied from war, parried the jingoists, tolerated anti-imperialists, and suffered the constant buffets of such "yellow journalists" as Joseph Pulitzer and William Randolph Hearst, whose newspapers created a national frenzy against Spanish terror in Cuba. McKinley tried to hold out but finally feared his party would demand war. He said, then, that he sought divine guidance.

Wreck of the battleship US *Maine,* sunk in Havana harbor, February 15, 1898, with some 260 killed. Loss of the *Maine* helped precipitate the Spanish-American War. Courtesy of the NARA, Department of Defense, Department of the Navy, Bureau of Ships.

This confession, distorted to a popular cartoon vision of the portly president on penitent knees, helped steer McKinley to ask Congress for neutral intervention in Cuba. Congress, on April 19, 1898, got ahead of the executive branch and empowered the president to use United States armed forces to free Cuba. On April 25 Congress declared war—but with an important caveat forced by the Teller Amendment, which prohibited the full annexation of the island.

McKinley's Civil War experience helped make him a strong war leader. Taking over the War Department when the secretary failed, supplies failed, and chaos replaced antique army organization, he soon supervised strategy, operations, logistics, and army-navy coordination, along with postwar policies. Victory came in a hundred days, after impressive U.S. naval victories in Cuba and the Philippines and such heroic land successes as Siboney, Daiquiri, Las Guasimas, San Juan Hill, and the capture of Santiago—all despite horrendous supply blunders born of incompetence and graft.

After the war McKinley sensed an imperialist urge in the country and moved swiftly to secure not only Cuba and Puerto Rico but also the Philippines, whose people the president wanted to "uplift." Hostilities ended with the Treaty of Paris (1899), under which Spain received $20 million, confirmed Yankee dominance in Cuba until independence, and abandoned all claims in Puerto Rico and the Philippines.

Unanticipated problems of military government in newly won territories expanded army administrative bureaucracy while an ongoing, stubborn

Elihu Root, secretary of war (1899–1904) under Presidents McKinley and Theodore Roosevelt. His reforms included the creation of a General Staff, a permanent increase in army strength, and joint planning by the army and navy. Courtesy of the Library of Congress.

Philippine fight for independence, led by charismatic leader Emilio Aguinaldo, made the army increasingly necessary. So, at the turn of the century, America's martial budget grew with recruiting and with a new generation of guns, munitions, ships, and supplies.

Facing the 1900 election, McKinley tried to control growing complaints about obscene military waste during the war by promising investigations and reorganization. To head army reorganization he turned to an unlikely man—Wall Street lawyer Elihu Root, who at first declined, pleading ignorance of martial matters. McKinley persisted and so appointed one of the greatest American war secretaries. Ignorance drove Root to deep studies of martial affairs, and in time his knowledge outstripped that of anyone else in government, including the generals. Soon he joined the president in urging military reforms that swept away the office of Commanding General of the Army (against incumbent General Nelson Miles's thunderous opposition), created the beginnings of a modern general staff headed by a chief who served as the secretary of war's military adviser, and fostered an Army War College. Professionalization of the officer corps, really begun by Commanding General William T. Sherman in the 1870s, expanded through an officially encouraged readership of such standard magazines as the *Cavalry Journal, Infantry Journal, Journal of the Military Service Institution of the United States,* and *Army and Navy Journal* along with other magazines publishing practical and scholarly material on ordnance and navy developments. Although the "Root Reforms" could not oust some entrenched staff bureau heads, they significantly modernized America's forces and provided a framework for waging bigger wars.

"Go Bind Your Sons to Exile"
—Rudyard Kipling, "The White Man's Burden"

International interests were certainly not new to the United States—but they had been minimized in a kind of echo to George Washington's farewell sermon against foreign attachments. Yet the strategic value of the Isthmus of Panama drew Yankee attention several times in the late nineteenth century, and continuing talk of a trans-isthmian canal fanned U.S. interest. Activist president Theodore Roosevelt conjured Panama's independence in 1903 and tucked it under U.S. protection.

Roosevelt, aware of the unstable finances in some of the Central and South American states, realized that foreign creditor nations could slip through an unexpected crack in the Monroe Doctrine. In collecting legitimate debts they could create financial protectorates—as illustrated by the Venezuelan crisis in 1902–1903. He acted quickly, telling Congress in his 1904 annual message that "chronic wrongdoing" or "impotence" by southern neighbors might force the United States to become an international police power—the United States would collect and remit foreign debts and stabilize currencies in the Americas. This so-called Roosevelt Corollary fixed American policy for several decades and encouraged a kind of paternalistic colonialism that affected such nations as Nicaragua and Mexico. Roosevelt wielded presidential wisdom and power eagerly in tending hemispheric affairs. Boasting "I took Panama," sea-power fan Teddy fashioned a large navy that he dispatched around the globe as proof America had come to stay.

Many prominent American anti-imperialists, including Mark Twain (whose satirical "Letter to the Person Sitting in Darkness" archly attacked expansion), guessed that a small taste of international power would bring gluttony. More, it brought a different kind of rationalization. Although Cuba would be independent, as America's protégé it required democratic reformation; its people, so long oppressed, needed physical nurturing and political guidance. Well reformed, Cuba would stand as a solid buckler of the Monroe Doctrine.

A rising vision of America's duty to spread democracy and stability on its cresting colonialism encouraged rationalizations that justified taking Puerto Rico and the Philippines—they, too, had suffered tyranny and deserved to have freedom thrust upon them.

Problems came with gluttony. Some dependencies refused to settle into prescribed routines. Philippine nationalists led by Emilio Aguinaldo resisted American

"Rough Rider" Col. Theodore Roosevelt, 1st Cavalry, U.S. Volunteers, c. 1898. Roosevelt had been assistant secretary of the navy (1897–1898) and would become vice president (1900–1901) and president (1901–1909). Courtesy of the Library of Congress.

occupation at the end of the Spanish-American War. A harsh war for independence raged until 1902 at a cost of 4,000 American and 20,000 Filipino warriors' lives, along with heavy civilian casualties. Early military governments established U.S. rule, which turned out to be fairly brutal—water torture, concentration camps à la Cuba, and frequent executions stained many American reputations in the islands. Slowly, though, civilian governors-general advanced Philippine progress on the road to independence. True peace never came to the islands: in the south, especially on the island of Mindanao and in the Sulu Archipelago, war continued. Warlike Moros, the Prophet's most eastern followers, ruled the southern areas and refused domination by Filipinos or anyone else.

Supposed democratic reforms in Cuba frayed in 1906 as an incumbent president there tried to rig his reelection. President Roosevelt, on his own, swiftly deployed 6,000 men as the United States took temporary control of the island's administration—until 1909. After that, various minor Yankee interventions generally kept peace in Cuba.

Woodrow Wilson, a cool, aloof political science professor, college president, and Democratic governor of New Jersey, came to the White House in 1912 in high hopes for a new, progressive domestic program, but he worried that fate might doom him to a war presidency. He preempted the possibility and became a moralistic interventionist—more active than his energetic predecessor, Teddy—determined to fashion a hemisphere of little democracies. That determination focused his early attention on Mexico, where revolution raged and General Victoriano Huerta had murdered his way to dictatorship. Legalist though he was, Wilson added his own corollary to the Monroe Doctrine as he began a policy of policing hemispheric politics. Declaring his determination "to teach the South American republics to elect good men," he refused to recognize Huerta's regime and offered aid to its enemies.

His first chance at petulant foot-stamping came on April 9, 1914, when a group of American sailors were arrested in Vera Cruz by a Huerista patrol for barging into a restricted zone. Despite profuse apologies from the Mexicans, the U.S. admiral commanding, demanded a twenty-one-gun salute to the Stars and Stripes. Almost gleefully, Wilson backed him up and asked for congressional approval to use force against Huerta. Congress stalled and no salute came.

Late in the month Wilson learned that a German ship approached the port of Vera Cruz with arms for Huerta, and this time he acted without appealing to Congress. On orders from Washington, 700 marines and sailors landed on April 21, and after a sharp fight took the town. Ten weeks later Huerta resigned, opening an era of Mexican upheaval. Gunboat diplomacy was alive and well.

Long-standing chaos in Haiti at last churned into a bloody civil war. The embassies of France and the Dominican Republic were raided, and American marines landed in July 1915 to stop the bloodbath and install a puppet president, Philippe Sudre Dartiguenave. Subservient to American interests, Dartiguenave accepted—virtually at gunpoint—a treaty that nearly gave his country to its new northern ally. Be it said for the United States that this episode caused some serious misgivings. "I confess," Secretary of State Robert Lansing wrote the president, "that this method of negotiation, with our Marines policing the Haytian [sic] capital is high-handed. It does not meet my sense of a nation's sovereign rights and is more or less an exercise of force and an invasion of Haytian independence. . . . [H]owever, I cannot but feel that it is the only thing to do if we intend to cure the anarchy and disorder which prevails in that Republic." Wilson answered pragmatically, "This, I think, is necessary and has my approval."[1]

High-handed Yankee policy certainly was, but it created a new and different Haiti that sported honest elections and reformed finances so that foreign debts were paid (which prevented European intervention). A kind of democracy was thrust upon the reluctant Haitians, and the marines stayed until after the Great War ended.

Much the same kind of occupation was endured by the Dominican Republic, which shared with Haiti the island of Hispaniola. After hectic years of Spanish, Haitian, then again Spanish rule to 1865, the Republic, lapsing into fiefdoms, barely held together. President Roosevelt had imposed customs reform in 1905. In 1914 President Wilson imposed political control by arranging new elections and installing a puppet president in October. Marines swiftly subdued an ensuing insurrection in 1916.

On the night of March 8–9, 1916, Pancho Villa's guerrillas raided Columbus, New Mexico. In a way this seemed a double outrage—Villa's banditry sullied an American town, yet his status as Mexican Robin Hood lent some sanctity to his violence. For President Wilson, however, the raid offered a chance to mix in the imbroglio between Villa and Mexican president Venustiano Carranza; Wilson favored Carranza but wanted him to clean up the border problems. Covered by an old Mexican-American treaty giving both parties the right of hot pursuit of bandits, Wilson ordered an army expedition to capture Villa and "put a stop to his forays." Since he was defending the United States against attack, and since he already had congressional approval for the earlier Vera Cruz incursion, Wilson did not bother asking approval of the famed "Punitive Expedition" commanded by Brig. Gen. John J. Pershing that rode into the state of Chihuahua on March 15, 1916. Everyone from Wilson to his new secretary of war, Newton D. Baker, and Army Chief of Staff Maj. Gen. Hugh Scott to Pershing himself hoped for a quick campaign; the longer it lasted, the more trouble was likely to come from Villistas and Carrancistas. It dragged on and troubles abounded.

Carranza's patience wore thin, his men harassed Pershing's columns, and a serious constitutional issue arose about prolonged invasion of a sovereign Mexico. As with Haiti, Wilson rose above his passion for national self-determination and ordered the expedition to keep after Villa. Pershing's men fought several hot skirmishes and a couple of serious battles that nearly caused war with Mexico. With Villa uncaught but weakened and the war in Europe building to world disaster, the Punitive Expedition finally returned to Texas in February 1917. Wilson's determination sustained some kind of principle and won a good deal of enmity for the truculent "Colossus to the North."

Wilson bought the Virgin Islands from Denmark and sent troops back to a simmering rebellion in Cuba in 1917. By the time America entered the Great War, the Caribbean was a Yankee ocean save for isolated islands controlled by Great Britain and France. Wilson had exported his own kind of loose colonialism at some cost to America's rectitudinous reputation.

6

The Great War

By the time Pershing's men returned to Texas, war had consumed Belgium and seeped across France into Italy and the Mediterranean basin, into Palestine, Turkey, Africa, most of the Balkans, and Russia. Great Britain barely survived as Germany's dreaded U-boats siphoned off food, arms, ammunition—all the wants of war and humanity. Most of Britain's supplies came from the United States, and by early 1917 the Atlantic lanes were dotted with sunken Allied and American ships.

President Wilson had been reelected in 1916 on the slogan "He kept us out of war"; moreover, he had tried to mediate between Germany and its Central Powers allies and the Franco-British Entente. From a lofty and truly idealistic neutrality he had urged the warring powers to achieve a "peace without victory"; to stop war before it became a grinding change agent too powerful to stop. No one took him up on a no-win peace, and U-boats increasingly flouted American neutrality. With each American life lost, Yankee tempers rose. When the German government arrogantly announced a renewal of unrestricted submarine warfare as of February 1, 1917, Wilson's temper flared. Confessing disbelief "that such things would . . . be done by any government," he proclaimed armed neutrality to Congress on February 26 and hoped that would alter German policy.

Nothing deterred the U-boat campaign. The Kaiser's High Command promised that submarines would starve Britain and her allies into submission before the hopelessly unprepared United States could get into the war. The Kaiser's government, nonetheless, wanted to keep the Yankees neutral; failing that, they planned a paralyzing diversion for the "Colossus to the North." All of this became clear to the American people on March 1, 1917. On that day, a Thursday, the stunning news earned national headlines. The *New York Times'* banner put it clearly enough: "GERMANY SEEKS ALLIANCE AGAINST U.S. ASKS JAPAN AND MEXICO TO JOIN HER." After that came the admission from Germany's foreign minister, Arthur Zimmerman, that this astounding report was true.

Americans seethed, and when U-boats sank three American ships on March 18 isolationists virtually vanished. On March 21 Wilson called Congress to a special session. On April 2 the tall, sober president who so cherished peace stood before a quiet audience. He recited the long, frustrating history of neutrality and then asked Congress to recognize recent German acts as constituting war against the United States. "It is a fearful thing to lead this great peaceful people into war," he said, "into the most terrible and disastrous of all wars. . . . But the right is more precious than peace and we shall fight for . . . democracy . . . and [to] make the world itself at last free." Congress voted for war on April 6, 1917, triggering a kind of national sigh of relief followed by rising tides of patriotism and pro-Allied sentiment.

Experiences in academe mixed with political rough and tumble taught the president much about his countrymen's character. He feared that Americans would not easily accommodate a massive mobilization of men, money, and regimentation. He guessed wrong. The people generally buckled down, accepting conscription and some minor privations, and rushed to provide all the sinews of war for the Allies and themselves.

Although his use of force in the Western Hemisphere showed he could be a strong commander-in-chief, Wilson really had an aversion to war and saw it as the curse of human failure. The war in Europe marked the worst failure, and the hecatombs sprawling in Europe's trenches were sacrifices to unreason. He felt America must fight to save something from catastrophe, and he vowed it should fight well.

Wilson understood the tragedies of war. He understood, too, that the Allies were nearly finished and that America's material and human help would have to arrive fast. How could America's aid be most effective? Wilson agreed with the idea that United States troops must soon appear in France, and he wisely turned war management over to his energetic war

Woodrow Wilson. Circumstances made it impossible for Wilson to honor his 1916 campaign slogan, "He kept us out of war." On April 2, 1917, he addressed Congress asking that it declare war on Germany. Four days later, the United States entered World War I. Courtesy of the Library of Congress.

secretary, Newton D. Baker. Consequently he accepted Baker's nomination of Maj. Gen. John J. Pershing to lead the Yanks abroad. Baker picked Pershing purely on his record—Pershing's father-in-law might be a prominent Republican senator, but the Punitive Expedition proved the general's mettle. Still suffering rigors of a terrible family loss in 1915 (his wife and three daughters died in a fire at the San Francisco Presidio; a son alone survived), the general soberly accepted the greatest challenge of his life. A brief visit with Wilson offered presidential confidence, and in meetings with Baker he found a flexible superior, dedicated supporter, and careful manager who deftly orchestrated America's mobilization of men, munitions, machines, camps, training, and shipping.

Everything was different about the European war. A relentless stalemate choked the front and blinded generals. Trench labyrinths in France had no precedent, no template—they were great maws consuming men and materiel and reeking of shells, gases, desolation, and doom. Most American images of the war came from headlines and scattered radio reports, and most of them were wrong. Reports, pictures, rumors, memories all paled in the realities suddenly brought home by Allied missions coming to beg help and tell why. Most of the glory was drowned in Flanders, and by 1917 even propaganda approached the truth.

Gen. John J. Pershing, General Headquarters, American Expeditionary Force, Chaumont, France, 1918. Courtesy of National Archives.

By the time Pershing and lead elements of the American Expeditionary Forces arrived in France, Russia tottered toward collapse—if that happened, Germany could bring about a million men to the Western Front. Allied leaders demanded bits and pieces of Pershing's forces for their depleted legions. He had carte blanche, though, from the president and Baker to form and use an American army; he held stubbornly to that objective. Deftly fending off allies, Pershing learned the new kind of war—a melange of men, trenches, airplanes, machine guns, fiendish gases, awesome artillery (one German cannon's range was more than seventy-five miles), awkward tanks, of sophisticated intelligence operations, of intricate logistics involving railroads, trucks, horses, medicines, and engineering—which depended on large and professional staffs.

Pershing's apparent selfishness in hoarding men infuriated such Allied leaders as Marshal Henri Pétain (hero of Verdun), Field Marshal Douglas Haig of the British forces, and their political superiors—who branded the Yank general nothing more than an old Indian fighter. But Wilson and Baker stayed steadfast; no complaints over Pershing's head went anywhere. Pershing learned and built his army. He gave generous help to the Allies during the nearly fatal German attack that began in March 1918—an attack to beggar all previous drives.

At dawn on March 21, 1918, 6,473 cannon shook the firmament of France and woke the prime minister in London. Silence came, suddenly shattered by 3,500 mortars at work closer to the front; then three newly refitted and reinforced German armies streamed out of the boiling mists. Seventy-one divisions—led by storm troops—rushed at the juncture of British and French armies near Amiens. Allied reserves were scarce, despite the long-watched gathering of General Erich Ludendorff's gray hosts, and in what seemed like minutes the British Fifth Army nearly evaporated. Germans swarmed toward Amiens; if Amiens fell, French plans were to concentrate southward and defend Paris while the British would gather at the coast for extraction across the Channel.

Two vital things happened, spurred by crisis. The Allies at last decided to make Ferdinand Foch supreme commander, and Pershing offered everything America had to stop the Germans—an action emotionally touted across both France and England. Slowly Ludendorff's legions halted, but he planned another attack on the Marne. American Marines and soldiers joined in hard fighting at Belleau Wood and Chateau Thierry. When Germany's great gamble to win in 1918 fizzled, Pershing created the First American Army and reduced the venerable St. Mihiel salient on the eastern shoulder of the French lines near Verdun. His September attack quickly proved that Yanks were fighters, and Foch shoved them into line in the frowning, dour Meuse-Argonne woods.

Foch and Marshal Pétain may have picked that heavily fortified place in expectation of failure. If so, they were nearly gratified. The initial attack on September 26 went well enough, and on September 27 the commanding eminence Montfaucon fell to the doughboys—but then enemy cannon and machine guns handled by veterans settled the attack into a bloody siege. Tough combat—small rushes for machine guns, ragged rushes for high ground, long, hard pushes for cannon east of the Meuse—sloughed away doughboys.

Careful reorganization, continual emphasis on an American army, won Pershing grudging Allied respect, and his army's victories coming out of the Argonne won their admiration, if not total appreciation. With a November armistice (opposed by Black Jack, who thought the Allies should march down the Unter den Linden), Pershing siphoned divisions home. He made mistakes and learned from them, and kept decent Allied relations. Most of all he had forged a United States Army that became a vital factor in victory.

American casualties had been heavy—no fewer than 120,000 dead, wounded, or gassed—but far less than others. Allied opinion soon saw America's effort as ancillary, if not a downright distraction to victory.

Americans at home bitterly resented the barely tolerant attitude of especially the British and French, who had so long borne the brunt of battle that they perceived Americans as poachers, as consumers of the war materiel they were supposed to provide; and when the big, healthy Yanks finally arrived, that stubborn Missourian kept them for himself, siphoned off a few for show during emergencies, but finally launched a fumbling attack against the already crumbling St. Mihiel salient. A good many Allied planes and guns were lent the Americans for this big debut. Kept, they were somewhat effectively used in the surprisingly successful early attacks in the Meuse-Argonne. But the snobbishness, the arrogance, the relegation of America to the status of a Portugal or a Belgium left a long and fresh resentment that lingered at least until World War II. Wilson's own snubbing of his men cut deeply among the doughboys, and they remembered.

Generalized Allied denigration came partly from jealousy of President Wilson's obtrusive prominence during the war—and also from his obvious dislike of martial matters. He had allowed U.S. participation in some north Russian operations to fight the Bolsheviks. His heart, though, lingered on peace. Failing interest in his peace without victory scheme, he had suggested in January 1918 ending the war on the basis of his Fourteen Points, which touched on territorial matters (secret treaties were already common gossip), "open covenants openly arrived at," disarmament, free trade sustained by freedom of the seas, self-determination of peoples, colonial adjustments, and, most of all, a League of Nations to maintain world amity.

Germany seized on Wilson's points as a basis for armistice; some Allies were irked at the territorial provisions; some were irked at the leniency and were reluctant adherents. Several small nations emerged from the peace conjured at Versailles. For Wilson the greatest tragedy came when his own nation rejected the League. He stumped the country for approval and failed. Shortly felled by a stroke, an embittered chieftain died in 1924. He deserves recollection, though, as a pragmatic idealist, anti-military but a strong and discriminating war leader.

"In Patience to Abide"

—Rudyard Kipling, "The White Man's Burden"

Most wars have messy endings—none more so than the "14–18 war." Wilson's pesky idealism required some respectful nods from the Allies while old rivalries and new angers among the victors fashioned a rancorous armistice that made a jigsaw-puzzle world. Colonies were handed around, some made independent, Wilson's self-determination brought a fillip of freedom to Hungary, Slovakia, the small Czech state; Poland grew slightly. Italy's representatives, fuming over Fiume, departed the negotiations. Japan grumbled at ultimately returning China's Shantung Province.

Most grumbling, both secret and blatant, swirled around Wilson's monotonous demand for a League of Nations to police peace. This academic fancy did a good deal of mischief since it gave small nations illusions of preservation and cramped future visions of the mighty. Reparations provisions depressed Wilson, who fought them in waning strength.

Wilson could not sell the League to the United States Senate, despite an exhausting, even heroic, swing around the country—isolationism redivivus, petty politics, budget worries after war's huge expenses shoved Wilson's dream beyond congressional concern. Deeply saddened, he watched the League limp along, full of enfeebled potential and riddled by shameless animosities.

While some of the victors began sharpening their colonial appetites, many of the defeated found peace worse than war. Germans, many feeling unbeaten but betrayed, saw stark ravages of defeat—their country wracked by hunger, saddled with war guilt, crushed by heavy reparations, its navy largely scuttled, its army held to 100,000 men without airplanes—and a deep, lingering anger took root far down in their loser's pride.

Some Allied leaders, including General Pershing, thought the victorious armies should have invaded Germany to make its citizens face defeat. Others felt that the heavy reparations demands—money, land, rolling stock, weapons, limits on armed services, a skeletonized navy—were almost enough to prevent more adventures by a future general staff.

With the Austro-Hungarian Empire gone, its surviving parts were unstable. Old Austria shrank to a kind of melodious city-state status, while newborn Hungary, battered by the 1920 Treaty of the Trianon, wallowed in stultifying inflation—rumors of wheelbarrow loads of paper money needed for a loaf of bread carried more truth than fancy.

Versailles's reverberations hardened terms of the 1920 Treaty of Sevres between Turkey and all Allies save Russia and the United Sates. The Ottoman Empire dissolved, Turkey lost Mesopotamia and Palestine, the Hejaz, Izmir, while Armenia became a republic.

Not all victors were happy. Spats among the Allies centered on scheduling of reparations, on disarmament, about who should fill France's trenches and save the land, about the League of Nations, and on war costs to beggar the world.

Nor was America immune. Distance exempted it from some local worries, but Allied demands for help escalated while the United States Congress decided that everything had cost too much; why the money hemorrhage abroad? "Helen Maria," Charles Dawes thundered before a committee. "We were fighting a war!" Realism from one of the army's best purchasing agents (and future U.S. vice president) breached an old parsimony—at least for a time. Many in Congress, though, argued that a peace dividend could be reaped by slicing military appropriations—the nation should go back to the comforts of little armies, few innovations, and serious doubts about airplanes. Protected by a carefully coddled fleet, America could huddle again behind its oceans. This happy whimsy won the obvious blessing of the "Roaring Twenties"—parched a bit by Prohibition.

As war fears dwindled a lingering bit of Wilsonian idealism led the United States into the Kellogg-Briand Pact of 1928, which outlawed war "as an instrument of national policy." Domestic wars disturbed the Flapper Age with gangsterism and a pitifully desperate "Bonus Army" of veterans who were rousted from Washington by U.S. troops.

Internal troubles plagued British politics as the Labour Party sought a tamed socialism. France splintered into a near infinity of political groups as it lurched right and left. Japan turned inward but the emperor held sway. Italy's king watched national politics wobble in the rise of a corporate state. Germany tried democracy as the Weimar Republic struggled out of the Hohenzollern ashes. Common to all the winners and losers was a deep, surging antiwar sentiment that surfaced in literary masterpieces of disillusion. Britain's poets Wilfred Owen and Julian Grenfell died in the war they etched, as did America's Joyce Kilmer. Such writers as Edmund Blunden, Robert Graves, Guy Chapman, and Romain Rolland recounted lost youth, lost future. America's Ernest Hemingway, Robert Sherwood, and John Dos Passos sketched war's parching of hope. Erich Maria Remarque's German classic *All Quiet on the Western Front* evoked the misery borne in the trenches. These works reflect not only martial cynicism but also a growing disenchantment with industrial munitions makers as "merchants of death."

Most people, winners and losers, wanted to believe that 1914–1918 had in-

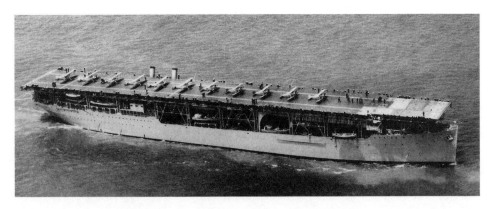

USS *Langley* (CV-1), originally the collier USS *Jupiter*, was converted into the U.S. Navy's first aircraft carrier and commissioned in 1922. This photo shows the *Langley* underway, with thirty-four planes on deck, June 1927. Courtesy of National Archives.

deed been "the war to end all wars." But an apocalyptic cavalry rode again in the 1930s and brought despair, poverty, unemployment, starvation.

When Wall Street crashed, so did much of the world's economy. Collapse of the massive loan structure that had propped up Europe since the war nearly bankrupted England, deranged France's industrialization, and wrecked the Weimar Republic. From the chaos Russia's Communists made smug inroads in Europe until Fascism's promises of stability installed dictators Benito Mussolini in Italy and Francisco Franco in Spain. Germany turned desperately right as baffled President Paul von Hindenburg made Adolf Hitler the nation's chancellor in January 1933. Hitler suspended the constitution of the Republic, made himself Fuhrer (leader), suppressed Communists, and put his Nazi (National Socialist German Workers) Party in charge of the Third Reich. Hitler's nationalist views fitted the wounded German psyche; his disavowal of Versailles, reoccupation of the Rhineland, and aggressive rearmament program sustained his pledge of progress.

In a sense Fascism snuck up on the democracies. Britain and France worried about Hitler (France built the Maginot Line in fear of renewed German aggression), but financial weakness combined with violent public pacifism forced them to a dithering diplomacy. Hitler was something of a pragmatist. Behind his ranting and his threats, he looked for strong objections to his program; he would have decamped from the Rhineland had France mobilized. Feckless opposition merely inflamed a latent Wagnerian dream, and he began a new expansionism first disguised as a drive for justice. Since Versailles's border outrages, he said, Austria languished in hope of redemption, as did a lost colony of Germans huddled in Czechoslovakia's Sudetenland. A carefully scripted coup regained Austria in March 1938, but Hitler had peace thrust upon him slightly later as Britain and France groveled away the Sudetenland at Munich in September.

Hitler scared most of Europe—his resurgent army cloaked in armor, legions craftily led by a nascent general staff, boasting a supposedly outlawed air force, his demands seemed to some modest enough. British prime minister Neville Chamberlain, no stranger to naïveté, announced "peace in our time" as he returned from Munich. In six months Hitler swallowed the rest of Czechoslovakia and protected his eastern flank with a Russo-German alliance.

There were some Western voices of warning in these craven years. From the ignominy of Parliament's back benches Winston Churchill's orations branded Hitler's Germany an infective evil presaging a new Dark Age. His reckonings of danger faded in the torpor of a wistful sort of hubris. France's obscure General Charles de Gaulle grasped the threat of German armor and tried to arouse a nation clinging to complacency and managed to dim his own career.

Franklin D. Roosevelt became America's president in 1932, in the deepest time of depression. He promised action, rushing emergency economic bills through a frightened Congress that finally resisted his galloping "socialism." Immersed in domestic crises, he nonetheless gave experienced attention to foreign affairs. Hitler he pegged a megalomaniac gorged on power. In the Far East he saw stirrings of a new Japanese imperialism that might threaten U.S. interests. Like his fellow Democrat Wilson, FDR hewed to peace, but not for the same reasons. Not only was the United States woefully unprepared for war—the army, hostage to poverty, had few men, fewer trained men, a straggle of competent officers, few planes; the navy had some good warships; America tolerated a few munitions manufacturers—but the country also wallowed in isolationism. Congressional Republicans saw American beaches as bulwarks and thought parsimony would end depression. Midst all this, farmers called for help, street-corner apple sellers showed a kind of last hope for capitalism, and an aristocratic president now proposed expanding the nation's debt to save it. FDR's options were thin, but he tried to expand them; his First Hundred Days legislative charge did bring some hope to all but the conservatives. He feared, looking abroad, that recovery would not match dangers circling democracy.

In September 1939 Hitler invaded Poland.

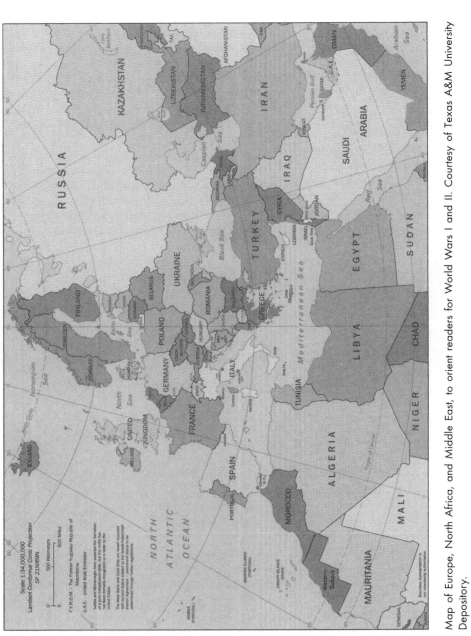

Map of Europe, North Africa, and Middle East, to orient readers for World Wars I and II. Courtesy of Texas A&M University Depository.

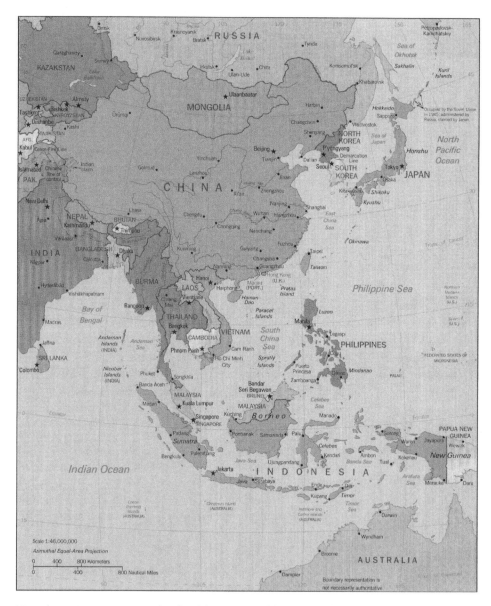

Map of East Asia, to orient readers for Philippines, World War II Pacific theater, and Korean and Vietnam conflicts. Courtesy of Texas A&M University Depository.

7

———————— • ————————

The Second World War

Most fortunately for the United States, President Roosevelt thrived on crisis. When Poland's guarantors, France and Britain, declared war against Germany on September 3, 1939, Roosevelt addressed Americans. He spoke of neutrality but expanded it to include profitable arms exportation and, in one of his famed fireside chats, observed that no government could command private sentiment—people could cheer for their side.

There is considerable historical argument about FDR's actions in 1939 and 1940. How serious was his neutrality? Didn't his relentless cheeriness cloak a secret heart for war? Or did his stirring speeches calling up pools of patriotism not go far enough, fast enough? Yes and no, for FDR's idealistic pragmatism let events lead his thoughts.

As the war seeped on, as Nazism, joined by Mussolini's Fascism, engulfed northern Europe, then France, his alarm grew. Prime Minister Winston Churchill's promise that Britain would wage "war against a monstrous tyranny never surpassed in the dark, lamentable catalogue of human crime" resonated in the White House. With Congress and much of the nation still mired in isolationism—even world hero Charles Lindbergh spoke of "America First"—Roosevelt began to make policy on his own. He traded fifty WWI destroyers to England for U.S. bases on various islands. When, at last, America began awakening to the world, FDR pushed supplying Britain with all kinds of war materiel through a Lend-Lease program—which may have saved the war. Although the Hitler-Mussolini Axis might well have made war over these actions, America clung to neutrality; military weakness still plagued and public opinion still dragged.

FDR addressed the weakness problem by a careful restructuring of the army's high command. Always looking for talent, Roosevelt appointed Gen. George C. Marshall as Army Chief of Staff in 1939 over many older heads. Marshall grew solidly into a job he soon defined.

Honesty and professionalism won Marshall wide congressional support as he began army expansion from 175,000 in 1939 to 1.4 million in 1941. Himself a victim of the army's entrenched seniority system, Marshall promoted carefully from among his personal list of skilled junior officers to make a modern force. Planning for large army expansion, he also did covert planning for a future U.S.-British alliance.

FDR, burgeoning dissimulator, talked of neutrality as he became increasingly convinced that the United States would have to go to war. He nudged ahead of home sentiments in December 1940 when he proclaimed that the United States must become the "arsenal of democracy." Still, increased war production did banish depression in a wave of recovery. Despite pledges to keep America's boys home, FDR seized on France's fall to support the Selective Service Act of 1940. Facing Europe's worsening war and Japan's flexing ambitions, he grew bolder. Hitler's sudden invasion of Russia in June 1941 offered a nearly miraculous respite to the West—but the Nazi juggernaut seemed unstoppable in its rush on Moscow.

As news of Hitler's general pogrom against Jews escalated, FDR knew that Churchill was right about the terrible threat the Nazis posed to democracy and to freedom. Terror stalked Germany as comprehensive efforts to exterminate all Jews in Europe spawned camps with gas chambers— Auschwitz, Dachau, and Sobibor among the worst—that fed murdered men, women, and children to ovens for disposal. Such human residue as gold from teeth, hair for mattresses, skin for gory lamp covers marked where millions of Jews had been. The Fuhrer had willing assassins running his genocidal program—Heinrich Himmler and Reinhard Heydrich set unprecedented standards of torture and terror. By the end of the war the Holocaust had consumed some 6 million Jews in a carefully planned example of man's inhumanity to man.

War events frightened America. Though war seemed inevitable, much of the nation hung on hopes for peace. Roosevelt had pressed to help the Allies about as hard as he could. Congressional isolationists' bitter attacks

President Franklin D. Roosevelt signing declaration of war against Japan, December 8, 1941. Courtesy of National Archives.

came almost daily. He wanted to help England, to help Russia, but he waited.

Japan's stirrings bothered FDR. He was probably not quite aware of the empire's economic distress as a trigger to resurgent expansionism. Japan faced serious raw materials shortages: the home islands could not even sustain a national ration of rice. The empire shattered illusions of seclusion in 1937. The staged "China Incident" covered a brutal invasion, including the mass terror of the "Rape of Nanking." China's long history of political disarray, of warlordism, its post-Boxer collapse beckoned exploitation. A new Chinese nationalistic government, though, fought hard, and Japan's adventure mired in a vastness of land and foreign malice.

President Roosevelt ranked among the most irked observers when Japan flowed into French Indochina, joined the Berlin-Rome-Tokyo Axis, and looked ready to engorge most of the Far East. He reacted with embargoes and in July 1941 froze Japanese assets in the United States.

On December 7, 1941, Japan attacked Pearl Harbor, Hawaii, sent fleets, planes, and armies swarming the Pacific, solved FDR's problems with pacifism, and began the end of World War II.

Historical conspiricists—they do exist—suspect that FDR maneuvered Japan's attack to get the United States in the war. If so, he would hardly have picked the chaotic Far East as the place to start. When he went before Congress on December 8 and asked for a declaration of war, and when, on December 11, Hitler inexplicably declared war on the United States, America's president knew the future had fallen on him. As more news sneaked out about Hitler's treatment of Jews, Allied victory became increasingly essential.

Plans are largely incidental in war, and events deranged America's Germany First strategy. Americans expected help for the Far East, especially for General Douglas MacArthur's little army in the Philippines. Nothing really could be done there; Pearl Harbor and dangling logistics denied aid as U.S. forces retreated to the Bataan Peninsula and finally surrendered at Corregidor in Manila harbor. MacArthur, ordered to Australia, called in righteous rhetoric for retribution.

FDR had watched as this war surged into a great scouring of everything. Most of what he knew of war management shifted in the facts, and he had to learn his own way of being commander-in-chief. Lincoln had commanded closely until he found his general; Wilson found Newton Baker and let him handle the war. Like Churchill, Roosevelt wanted to tinker with things naval, but he brought redoubtable Henry L. Stimson back to his old job as secretary of war. Stimson and Marshall made a team that meshed smoothly with the president and Navy Secretary Frank Knox.

Too much an activist to leave the war all to generals and admirals, Roosevelt kept a close eye on American and Allied action. George Marshall briefly feared micromanagement, but learned to work easily with a chieftain whose steady vision was victory. As he grew into the war, FDR grew

When completed in January 1943, the Pentagon was the world's largest office building, composed of five concentric buildings connected by corridors, covering thirty-four acres. It houses the headquarters of the U.S. Department of Defense. Courtesy of the Library of Congress.

beyond it. Aware that diplomacy embraced global strategy, Roosevelt went to all the Allied conferences, listening, largely agreeing with Churchill as Britain bore the brunt. The president's boldness grew with America's strength. He kept Pacific strategy in his, MacArthur's, and the navy's hands, which Churchill's pragmatism acknowledged—although the prime minister bridled at America's tenacious support for Chiang Kai-shek's corrupt Nationalist government. FDR slowly inserted veteran U.S. officers into European commands. It would be an American, Gen. Dwight D. Eisenhower, who commanded the invasion of France in 1944.

Congress, ridden still by many die-hard conservatives, bent to the chief executive's dedication. Actually Congress got ahead of him before the United States entered the war and voted more money than he thought he could expect; after Pearl Harbor and initial fumblings in North Africa, he took control of a grateful Congress. What he asked for to win, he got— sometimes with bonuses.

Domestically things were tough for FDR. Republicans and some dissident Democrats blundered early with a partisan investigation of the administration's "loyalty." Finally, they abandoned attacking a popular war leader and shifted to slamming some of his appointees. And they caught him out on some things important to him. Vowing to avoid the World War I precedent of curbing civil liberties, the president had, in the late 1930s, ordered the Federal Bureau of Investigation to look suspiciously at some strong German and Axis communities. The Congress, sensing uncertainty, and in the name of national security, reenacted the World War I Espionage Act and an Alien Registration Law that allowed the government actively to expose "disloyal" Americans and begin denaturalizing Nazi sympathizers. Fortunately for the president and the country, Attorney General Francis Biddle opposed these laws and secured Supreme Court modifications in 1944.

War hysteria and politics often dilute presidential ideals. Sincere as he may have been about the Constitution, FDR subverted it and enshrined an ugly American imperium in 1942. On February 19 he signed an executive order rounding up and deporting to inland "relocation" camps some 120,000 West Coast Japanese, over half of whom were American citizens. German Americans and Italian Americans largely escaped such tainting. Congress ratified FDR's order, and the Supreme Court skirted around the worst invasion of civil liberties to that time.

Such ignominious action Congress certainly understood and might have forgiven, but when FDR began creating offices, committees, "administrations" to run around them, congressmen took aim at his cherished

Dwight D. Eisenhower, five-star General of the Army, Supreme Commander Allied Forces in Europe, at his headquarters, European theater, 1945. Future president (1953–1961). Courtesy of National Archives.

New Deal, dismantled some it in the name of enhancing the war, and kept up a tiresome sniping.

Sniping, however, generated some bad politics, especially after the president swept the nation's radios with humorous rebuttals mixed in soaring words of hope. Congress had, finally, to hold its dignity as it sustained FDR's war.

Why not? Even critics admitted he did so much, so well. By the end of 1943 the country felt good about winning—it would take time, but the Allies would win. The whole country was mobilizing. Colonel Oveta Culp Hobby, first director of the Women's Army Corps (WAC), described the nation's mood in a tribute to the women who served: "Women who stepped up were measured as citizens of the nation, not as women. . . . This was a People's War, and everyone was in it."[1] The country felt good about FDR, too; it took pride in his gifted "conferencing" and felt partnership in his diplomacy. At the end of another year, people could see the obvious stresses of polio and his job but counted on an indomitable strength staying in him.

Strategically his views were generally sound. He left most of the European operations to Churchill and steadily supported Marshall and Eisenhower. Though once afraid of MacArthur's power, FDR approved of his island-hopping from New Guinea toward the Philippines. And from Pearl Harbor's anguish he watched a refitted U.S. Navy, heavy now with carriers and planes, cut Japan off from its resources and sink the Imperial fleets.

America's foreign policy remained essentially self-serving. War on a world scale seemed to many conservatives at home an unnatural diversion from the long tradition of the Monroe Doctrine. When the war ended the United States should go back to minding its own business. In keeping with long tradition, rapid demobilization was planned to follow the war.

FDR knew, though, that there really was no going back. As he capitalized on America's waxing power, he realized that the country would have to prop up peace in the world for some time. Like his idealistic predecessor Wilson, Roosevelt sought an international body to share problems of peace-keeping. He echoed nearly Wilsonian notions of an international system of security in the August 1941 Atlantic Charter discussions with Churchill. Even in war's early uncertainties he became a relentless advocate of a United Nations organization to prevent future wars.

Making the end of the war, though, seemed the most difficult problem facing the Allies as victory loomed. Stalin's truculence paced Red armies rushing through Bulgaria, Romania, Hungary, Austria, deep into the Third Reich; and he pressed for keeping what Red forces won. FDR soft-pedaled Churchill's oft-voiced suspicions of "Uncle Joe's" plans for a Soviet Europe. In one of his worst misjudgments, America's president believed that he could handle Stalin—a boast hardly sustained at earlier Allied conferences. By the time FDR, Churchill, and Stalin—the Big Three—met at Yalta in February 1945, America's chief executive had lost none of his political charm, but waning physical strength and fatigue thinned his influence. Stalin's armies gave him control of the meeting, and he proved adamant in demanding heavy German reparations against FDR's objections, adamant, too, about Poland's borders and France's influence. The Soviet leader did agree with the Teheran Conference decision to create a United Nations, largely because he seemed to fear Western pressure to "rule the world." He did agree, too, to war against Japan after Germany's defeat, and won concessions in the Far East at both Japan's and China's expense. Churchill lamented FDR's concessions as merely feeding Stalin's greed; the "sellout" of Poland badly bothered him.

Reporting to Congress on Yalta, FDR (weakened to sitting in a wheel-chair) confessed that if America failed to sustain the Yalta agreements, the whole structure of postwar Europe might collapse. He met quick criticism for giving away too much at Yalta, though public opinion sustained his drive for the UN. Be it said for him that he confessed Yalta's weaknesses but argued that he got the best results he could. Still, only a raving optimist could find virtue in a weaseling of Western conscience.

President Roosevelt died before the end—at Warm Springs, Georgia, on April 12, 1945—before the Atomic Age erupted at Hiroshima in August, before the UN convened, and before the fullest threat of Stalinism.

Historians have generally been kind in assessing FDR's war leadership. Effective—certainly, more than most he ranks as the engineer of victory. Astute politician—absolutely, with some expedient lapses of principle. National leader—surely, the conscience of a cause. Fewer accolades go to his late diplomatic leadership, where hubris, wistfulness, and infirmity stunted his vision.

Perhaps his repute should rest on being America's first constitutional monarch; a leader daring, even gleeful, in power. True, he followed the trail of a growing imperialistic war presidency but blazed it differently; he gathered to him all tokens of authority and made the White House the international fulcrum of war. Above all he knew that the United States had irrevocably joined the world, and started it toward the role its power demanded.

The Truman Doctrine

Americans looked at their new president with hope and some disbelief. What most knew about Harry S Truman hardly inspired: a former Missouri farmer and haberdasher, WWI veteran, political creature of the infamous Democratic Pendergast machine of Kansas City who made it to the U.S. Senate in 1934—where he had cut his own course and done well. During the war he headed a committee that uncovered waste in defense spending and saved some $15 billion while speeding war production. A compromise selection as FDR's vice president in 1944, Truman met Roosevelt only twice in the eighty-three days of his tenure and knew virtually no state secrets—including the atomic bomb project. Although he had high respect in the Senate, the country barely knew him. On April 12, 1945, he took the oath as president of the United States.

No stranger to hard work and a surprisingly quick study, Truman helped organize the United Nations charter signing in San Francisco in late April and on May 8 proclaimed V-E (Victory in Europe) Day as Germany surrendered.

With Japan nearly a burning wreck, an Allied conference would convene in Potsdam, a suburb of ruined Berlin, to implement the controversial Yalta decisions. Stalin would come, as would Churchill (with Clement Attlee), as well as the new American president. Truman prepared to fight some of FDR's Yalta concessions but went to the meeting anxiously awaiting news of the atomic bomb test in Los Alamos, New Mexico. As the Big Three gathered, Stalin held the strongest position: Red Army troops controlled Eastern Europe, and even the meeting place where the conference convened, Cecillienhof Palace, stood close to an ancient Russian settlement. Churchill's strength was threatened by an imminent election which Attlee seemed likely to win; Truman appeared uncertain in such heady realms.

What to do about Germany and Austria headed the official agenda along with questions about Poland and some Eastern European nations under Russian occupation. Almost from the start distrust wafted in the wings as Stalin's bluster seemed to seal his grip on Europe. Churchill, whose suspicions were wise, sought Truman's aid in trimming Yalta's writ to the Red dictator. Truman, timid and hesitant, hung back, and Churchill guessed why—the president waited for news about the bomb. When Truman's flat Missouri tones turned tough after a couple of days the prime minister knew that America's atom bomb worked. Designed to subdue Hitler and Hirohito, the bomb suddenly gave the United States unimaginable power. Truman's vague comment to Stalin about a new and deadly weapon (not unexpected) brought the stolid hope that the United States "would make good use of it." Still, things got easier after the announcement, and some of Yalta's concessions were modified in heated arguments.

While the delegates struggled through discussion of European boundary lines, Churchill and Attlee journeyed to England's election. Attlee returned to Potsdam as the new prime minister and supported Truman's views. Finally from the meeting came the Potsdam Agreement, which announced the victors' plans for Europe—Germany and Austria sliced into four occupation zones (the French got a slice of Britain's and America's shares), with Berlin and Vienna similarly carved, while Poland's German border would run along the Oder-Neisse Line. The Soviet Union would join the war against Japan in mid-August (Stalin saw rich Far Eastern opportunities).

Such touchy issues as reparations and individual peace treaties were handed off to committees. The end of the conference was marked by growing arguments about Soviet-occupied areas and democracy.

About a week before the conference's end, the Potsdam Declaration, sponsored by the United States, Britain, and China, called upon Japan to surrender uncondi-

President Truman ordered a second atomic bomb, nicknamed "Fat Man," dropped on Nagasaki, Japan, August 9, 1945. The plutonium implosion device produced a mushroom smoke column that rose over 60,000 feet in the air. Courtesy of the Library of Congress.

tionally or face "the utter destruction of the Japanese homeland." Japan announced that it would *mokusatsu* (kill with silence) the declaration. On his way home Truman ordered an atomic bomb dropped on Japan. The first one fell on Hiroshima on August 6, a second on Nagasaki on August 9; Emperor Hirohito accepted Potsdam's terms on August 14, and the war ended.

On March 5, 1946, Westminster College in Fulton, Missouri, conferred an honorary degree on Winston Churchill. After receiving the degree, the former prime minister gave a tough speech about the transformation of Europe: "From Stettin in the Baltic to Trieste in the Adriatic an iron curtain has descended across the Continent," he said, and described the relentless march of Soviet power, not only in Europe but wherever Communist parties grew. A firm alliance between the English-speaking peoples, Churchill thought, could save democracy. Stalin fumed and Soviet policies hardened in the UN. The "Iron Curtain" speech possibly marked the start of the Cold War.

Time confirmed Churchill's declaration. President Truman watched the USSR's growing greed and knew that surviving democracies needed help. He knew, too, that he headed the only nation strong enough to preserve the fruits of victory. A near-bankrupt Britain had received a large loan in 1946 as it brutally trimmed its foreign commitments, including aid to strife-torn Greece and unstable Turkey. Threatened Soviet control of Middle Eastern oil could push a teetering Europe to collapse.

On March 12, 1947, Truman unveiled a plan to aid free nations struggling against Communist infiltration. Congress heard him ask for $400 million that day because "I believe that it must be the policy of the United States to support free peoples who are resisting attempted subjugation by armed minorities or by outside pressures. I believe that we must assist free peoples to work out their own destinies in their own way. I believe that our help should be primarily through economic and financial aid which is essential to economic stability and orderly political processes. . . . We must take immediate and resolute action." By declaring America's concern for the free world, the Truman Doctrine changed the course of United States foreign policy—it scrapped the Monroe Doctrine and confirmed America's global opposition to communism.

Still, Soviet expansion continued, and in June 1947 the United States offered the Marshall Plan to stimulate European recovery and invited the USSR's participation. Stalin declined and pressured satellite nations to do the same. The program announced by Secretary of State George C. Marshall provided some $13 billion to sixteen countries from 1948 to 1952; succeeding beyond expectations, the plan changed the history of Europe as it sustained an emerging strategy of containing Communist infiltration.

Fearful of fancied American economic imperialism, the USSR picked jointly occupied Berlin as a point of counterattack. Late in June 1948 Red Army forces blocked the roads and railroads from the west into the city. Reacting carefully, the Allies organized a supply airlift that sustained West Berlin's people for 322 days. Allied determination and ingenuity ended the blockade and fended off war.

Successful blockade running reinforced Truman's notion that the Soviets respected force. And as Communist regimes controlled or threatened Czechoslovakia, East Prussia, Estonia, Latvia. Lithuania, Poland, Romania, Finland, Albania, Bulgaria, and Hungary, the president expanded the Truman Doctrine into military areas and began a revival of America's martial strength. When, in March 1948, five European nations formed a mutual military assistance organization to resist the USSR, Truman followed a congressional resolution and in April 1949 helped create the North Atlantic Treaty Organization (NATO), which committed European members, Canada, and the United States to defend Western Europe. NATO marked the first peacetime military alliance for the United States since the Franco-American pact of 1778. First headquarters were in France, and the first Supreme Allied Commander in Europe was Gen. Dwight Eisenhower.

Hiding behind the nuclear umbrella looked safe enough as Soviet seepage slowed, but the policy spawned a dangerous hubris—the United States began its own kind of expansion under the guise of containment. In the summer of 1949 balances shifted sharply as the USSR exploded an atomic bomb over Siberia, Communists drove the Nationalists out of China, and the USSR and the People's Republic of China formed an alliance. A hurried push to rearmament and production of a hydrogen bomb backed a U.S. announcement of a new Asian "defense line" including the Aleutian Islands, Japan, the Ryukyu Islands, and the Philippines. Nationalist China worried at the exclusion of Taiwan. A good many American martial minds worried that the country had bitten off more commitments than it could chew. The Bomb made slicing the defense budget a kind of congressional game, and much time was needed for military recovery.

On Sunday, June 25, 1950, just ahead of daylight, troops of the Soviet-backed Democratic People's Republic of Korea invaded the Republic of Korea to the south. Banking on American inability to help its southern puppet, the northern Communist regime determined to destroy the fictional ROK and unify the peninsula.

All odds ran against the South in spite of American friendship: utterly surprised, its poorly trained army, lacking tanks, artillery, and aircraft, fragmented against well-trained divisions supported by artillery, 120 Soviet T-34 tanks, and 180 planes. Quickly across the 38th parallel, northern troops were nearly in Seoul, the South's capital, before the rest of the world knew what was happening.

8

•

Korea

"The toughest decision I had to make as president."

—Harry Truman[1]

He enjoyed family time with his wife and daughter, he enjoyed his early morning walks, and he relished playing the piano for White House guests; these happy domestic niceties almost cloaked Truman's strengths. Old Missouri political friends saw a deep-struck independence beneath his machine-made success. Buddies from World War I artillery duty remembered his energetic courage; Senate colleagues knew his toughness on the floor and in committee. So they were only moderately surprised at his grit in Potsdam's testing, at the bluntness of the Truman Doctrine, his thwarting of the Berlin blockade, his nurturing of NATO—all this showed a flexible mind in an iron will.

Both will and flexibility were jolted on June 25, 1950, when the Communist Democratic People's Republic of Korea (DRK) invaded South Korea in an avalanche of troops, guns, and planes. Republic of Korea (ROK) forces fragmented, abandoned their paucity of equipment, and ran. With news of the invasion Truman faced traumatic crises of conscience, conflict, time, distance, and consequences. With typical pragmatic determinism—in what he termed the hardest decision of his presidency—Truman scrapped tradition, largely bypassed the Constitution, and found his own way of launching war by using the UN.

Pushing a Security Council (fortunately being boycotted by the USSR) resolution calling for DRK withdrawal and another demanding help from member nations, Truman, without congressional approval, ordered all available U.S. forces in the area to aid the ROK. He had serious qualms: that the Soviets, allies of North Korea, might counterattack by grabbing Europe. Failure to aid the ROK, though, would dishonor an alliance, weaken the UN, possibly encourage China to seize Taiwan and threaten the whole Pacific Rim.

He did, on June 27, tell Congress and the world that U.S. forces would help the ROK. Communist spread in Asia had to be stopped, he said. He triggered a national tropism by adding that "we know that what is at stake is nothing less than our national security and the peace of the world." Congress cheered, although some members opposed using the UN as a way for the president to launch a war he persisted in calling a "police action." World reaction varied when Truman became executive agent for the UN's Korean crusade and appointed MacArthur as Commander-in-Chief, United Nations Command, which transmogrified into CINCUNC.

General MacArthur's men were too few and too ill-equipped to make a quick difference in Korea. Eighth Army, his main force under Lt. Gen. Walton Walker, mustered four understrength divisions and a combat team, all dismally short of armor, artillery, ammunition, and other supplies. Organized and equipped for air defense, most U.S. planes were short-range jet fighters hardly useful for close ground support. The navy counted five combat ships without much of an amphibious capability—but the Seventh Fleet was close.

Shocked by what he saw on a visit to Korea, MacArthur reported that Seoul fell on June 28 and the ROK Army had scrambled across the Han River. There DRK units regrouped for a drive toward the south and the strategic port of Pusan on the southeastern tip of the peninsula. Piecemeal deployment is not tactically sound, but MacArthur had no choice if he wanted U.S. troops in action. By early July, North Koreans held Kimpo airfield and the port of Inchon. By dawn on July 5, U.S. Task Force Smith, a sacrificial unit of 540 men, sat astride a main road toward Pusan; attacked by a division with thirty-three tanks, the Yanks fought hard, knocked out four tanks, and killed or wounded 127 enemy soldiers. Shortages of anti-tank rockets and other ammunition cost 150 American men and brought a disorganized American retreat. Still weak in men and materiel, U.S. forces tried three more rueful delaying actions.

As numbers of other UN nations joined the battle, Lt. Gen. Walton Walker took command of all U.S. and ROK ground troops on the peninsula and put his headquarters at Taegu at the Kum River. Flanked again, Walker, in August, pulled back to an arc protecting the port of Pusan — there he determined to stay.

Logistics often frustrates field commanders. Cold logistical logic holds that the force closest to its base has a potential edge. As U.S. supplies built up from Japan, Walker's situation bettered, while North Korean troops found themselves increasingly strangled by long and exposed supply lines. Expecting that possibility, MacArthur reached back to his South Pacific amphibious campaigns and dabbled in strategy.

It is not demonstrably true that there are old commanders and bold commanders but no old, bold commanders. At seventy MacArthur looked and acted fifty; the new war deducted ten years from that, and he thrived on the biggest challenge of his military life. His army's back to the sea, resources flimsy, threats daily and prospects dim, he confronted the Joint Chiefs of Staff with a stunning return to the basics — outflank the enemy and win the war.

Much paper rattling and hand wringing occupied the Pentagon at the general's proposal to land at Inchon, nearly 250 miles up the western Korean coast, cut inland, capture Seoul, and choke off the enemy's retreat. Objections oozed from committee wisdom — Inchon was too far, horrendous tides exposed huge mud flats, the city surely had tough defenses, the whole landing force might be stranded between city and sea. Even the general's worshipful staff — especially naval experts — balked a bit. MacArthur pushed planning, had weather and tides plotted and replotted, and ordered an amphibious landing by the new X Corps on September 15; on September 29 American troops reached Seoul, the choke point for most north-south roads and railroads.

Finally Walker broke out of the Pusan perimeter, and the enemy, aware of Seoul's fall, fragmented in a sudden panic northward. U.S. forces moved inland from Seoul, and in a few weeks most of the North Korean Army surrendered as UN troops neared the 38th parallel.

With 100,000 prisoners and DRK remnants in flight before him, MacArthur sensed a moment to exterminate the enemy. He pushed Washington for permission to press on across the 38th parallel and mop up. President Truman and the JCS hesitated; China and the USSR had vaguely threatened action if the UN entered North Korea. Despite the possibility of Russian or Chinese intervention, Truman gave the go-ahead. In early October General Walker sent three columns across the parallel, and within three weeks advanced over 200 miles, captured the North Korean capital of P'yongyang, cleared out most North Korean stragglers, and neared the Manchurian border. Another amphibious landing by the X Corps on the northeastern Korean coast at Wonson swept up the industrial areas on the coast and also headed for Manchuria.

On October 3, a direct Chinese threat to enter the war if non-ROK forces crossed the line was ignored in the hubris of victory. As rising unease, though, spread in the White House, Congress, and even the UN, the president called MacArthur to an October 15, 1950, meeting at Wake Island. Almost everything worked against Truman when they met. MacArthur's awesome reputation and his arrogant confidence preempted the agenda and snatched the cameras' eyes. An upstaged president asked if the general took the Chinese threat seriously. No, came the answer, followed by firm predictions of total success. The president, bolstered by another UN resolution, shifted the objective from restoring South Korea to unifying the peninsula. So the advance continued, with CINCUNC's satrapy confirmed.

Walker's Eighth Army worked into a mountain country whose valleys spread UN forces like a splaying hand. Walker not only had to scrap concern about mass and security but also had to worry about North Korea's creeping glacial winter. While MacArthur had hoped to end the war before winter, supply agencies did herculean duty in providing warm clothing and hot rations as American troops strayed farther apart in a puzzling enemy wilderness.

Although increasingly worried about Walker's dispersion, the U.S. Joint Chiefs of Staff hesitated to give tactical orders and tried to maneuver the president into direct command. MacArthur's mystique held as he ignored a directive to send only ROK troops close to Korea's Chinese and Russian borders and ordered an attack to win the war by Christmas. Releasing each Eighth Army column to advance as fast and as far as possible, MacArthur virtually dissolved Walker's front and waited for spot news from the Yalu River.

Good news came in bits and dribbles: an ROK regiment reached the town of Chosan on October 26 and scouted the river. Bad news came in waves and torrents as UN forces everywhere else stalled and found themselves fighting masses of Chinese "volunteers" who had mysteriously entered the war. The Chinese—number estimates varied, but the battle odds approached five to one—twice deliberately broke contact with UN forces. These possible hints at truce lines were ignored in a miasma of uncertainty everywhere except CINCUNC's headquarters. Certainty prevailed there through November: the Chinese objectives were defensive. UN forces resumed the attack in mid-November, gained ground, and perched one division on the Yalu River once again.

A massive Chinese attack at the end of the month surprised MacArthur, and Walker's hasty retreat degenerated into a near rout as he pulled back toward the 38th parallel. While the Eighth Army retreated, the X Corps fought toward the east coast. The 1st Marine Division and parts of the 7th Division, surrounded at the Chosin Reservoir, began a grim, heroic six-day march in −25°F cold toward Hungnam. Of the 15,000 who started the march, 4,400 were casualties and most of the rest frostbitten when they reached the sea.

Humiliated, MacArthur fancied revenge—even using the Bomb—but President Truman launched a spoiling diplomatic attack. Prime Minister Clement Attlee and Truman met in the first week of December to talk about the world situation. Fears that the Soviets might use Korea to cover overrunning Europe haunted the meeting. Both leaders had mobilized a good many men against that possibility (the United States called almost 3 million men), and Korea's sporadic crises had to stop. From the meeting came another presidential change of objective—stop trying to unify Korea and, once behind a defensible line, negotiate a way out of the war.

MacArthur received stiff orders to the strategic defensive, no reinforcements and a new 8th Army commander, Lt. Gen. Matthew B. Ridgway: the able Walton Walker died in a truck accident just before Christmas. Reverses continued, and in early January 1951 Seoul fell again to the enemy; but by April UNC forces again crossed the 38th parallel and dug in.

In March President Truman sent CINCUNC a draft copy of an offer to negotiate with the Chinese and North Koreans. MacArthur took this pusillanimous proposal as confirmation of a spineless chief executive. He broadcast his own belligerent demands for enemy surrender, thereby preempting presidential authority, causing considerable confusion about who was running the UN Korean effort, and plumbing Truman's Missouri patience. That patience vanished in April with MacArthur's public reply to a congressman's query about the war. Standing firm in Korea, the general opined, would prevent communism's spread in Europe as well as Asia. Proclaiming no substitute for victory, he astoundingly urged unleashing Chiang Kai-shek's Nationalists, which would have brutally widened the war.

President Harry Truman signing declaration
of national emergency, December 16, 1950.
Courtesy of National Archives.

The president relieved MacArthur of all his duties on April 11, 1951, and gave the command to General Ridgway. This tardy move stunned the American public and some UN allies.

When the USSR proposed a truce, both sides sat down to an ugly, niggling puzzling of how to settle issues from protocol to prisoners. Not until July 1953—after Gen. Dwight D. Eisenhower became the U.S. president—did an armistice go into effect—roughly along the 38th parallel—which still maintains something like the *status quo ante bellum*. UN losses came to 88,000 killed, over 23,000 of which were Americans. Total UN casualties were daunting: 460,000, 300,000 of them South Korean.

What of MacArthur? He returned to a Roman triumph, to wild greetings in New York and other cities, addressed a joint session of Congress, and made an eloquent recessional before West Point's Corps of Cadets. A Great Captain? Nearly. Gifted, daring, often unconventionally successful, he never controlled his own conceits.

What of Truman? A strong president, yes, but a weak one for warring. Certainly he was right in his "toughest decision" to save South Korea and in sticking to his global strategy of Communist containment. But in war, too soft too often, a vacillator who frequently confused colleagues and subordinates, he virtually invited Korea's command absurdities. He did, though, sustain the UN's peacekeeping mission while also greatly strengthening NATO.

"Peace Itself Is War in Masquerade."
—John Dryden, "Absalom and Achitophel"

And peace came—an uncertain, wobbly kind of long armistice that tested patience and drained exchequers. For the United States it brought puzzles about facing a future of increasing liability for democracies everywhere. Truman pondered continuation of his doctrine while the Defense Department pondered lessons from Korea. Obviously the intelligence community needed upgrading, both in talent and in acceptance by the senior military. Obviously, too, since a number of World War II aircraft provided saving tactical air support to the 8th Army and X Corps, some different kinds of jets were needed. American artillery again proved itself both skilled and essential in field operations—but more and nimbler guns would be needed in whatever wars would come. Korea provided comforting evidence of the marvels of U.S. logistical capacity; on the other hand, it showed how far tactical aptness had declined in a deliberately minimized army. The resulting rebuilding restored capacity as well as confidence.

America's vulnerability to nuclear attack had nearly mesmerized the Defense Department since Hiroshima. The hobgoblin of a "nuclear winter" helped create the Strategic Air Command (under redoubtable Gen. Curtis LeMay) in the late 1940s with the mission of explosive retaliation to any atomic assault.

Confidence dominated the American presidential election of 1952. Indecision in Korea, the draggling peace negotiations, and the sheer loom of the Republican candidate, Dwight D. Eisenhower, foredoomed Adlai Stevenson. Ike, as everybody knew him, promised to end the stalemate. Going to Korea as president-elect, he ate with the troops, surveyed the people and the ground, and decided that the war was unwinnable. The question was how to push the Communists to an armistice. Shipping to Korea a huge cannon that fired new tactical nuclear shells, a vow to sustain the ROK, together with the death of Joseph Stalin in March 1953, combined to break the cease-fire logjam in July.

Predictably, the presidency limited Ike's options. Martial realist that he was, he recognized that America's future foreign policies would be sustained by heavy use of force; the military must share in global planning. Determined to stick by the Truman Doctrine, Ike nonetheless resisted the idea of sinking into more small wars. Although not entirely happy with it, Ike supported the "New Look" in U.S. strategy foisted upon the Pentagon by Secretary of State John Foster Dulles—each and every threat would be met by "massive retaliation," he said, in what amounted to Truman's old program of nuclear deterrence redivivus. If it had failed to deter the North Koreans and their allies in 1950, how effective could it be with the USSR now buttressed by its own large atomic arsenal? Skewed it may have been, but massive retaliation remained America's main war strategy throughout Ike's administration. The now independent air force concentrated on expanding its vaunted capacities in strategic bombing as the main bulwark against attacks on America, and the navy focused on submarine-launched Polaris nuclear missiles.

Be it said for Ike that he tried to shore up his uncertainty with a serious effort to strengthen the economy, energize the nation's infrastructure, and revive patriotism to sustain the nation in the face of possible nuclear horrors. Still, cuts in the defense budget were alarming enough to trigger resignations of such distinguished generals as Matthew Ridgway, Maxwell Taylor, and highly promising Lt. Gen. James M. Gavin.

Ridgway protested that when nuclear parity came, the USSR could foment small wars that constricted U.S. forces could not meet. Taylor, Gavin, and a number of civilian scholars shared a general fear that America's restrictive strategy might make total nuclear war unavoidable. Finally, when nuclear parity arrived—even in thermonuclear bombs—as the 1950s ended, Americans worried that massive retaliation would beget the same in a holocaust of extermination. Slowly the United States and the USSR shared the view that nuclear weapons should be "the last and not the only recourse."[2]

Still, the nuclear arms race kept going, and tensions escalated. At Geneva in 1955 the Soviets agreed to avoid atomizing the world. Pressure eased, although Russian premier Nikita Khrushchev did promise to help in national liberation wars against capitalism. Ike, suspecting massive retaliation's coming obsolescence, and concerned about continental defense, beefed up U.S. radar early warning efficiency and pushed air force and army development of self-delivered long-range and intermediate range missiles as well as air defense systems.

Rudely, Russia broke the parity stalemate in 1957, first with an operational intercontinental ballistic missile (ICBM), then with Sputnik, the first space satellite, which emboldened a firmer hold on its puppet states. These alarms triggered a U.S. crash program in rocket fuels and vehicle design as the so-called Cold War reached near critical mass.

Seriously worried about the USSR, about strengthening NATO's chances to protect Europe, as well as SEATO's (Southeast Asia Treaty Organization) hope of holding Taiwan and fending communism's growth, the president was suddenly jolted by an unwelcome resurgence of Middle Eastern troubles.

Eisenhower should hardly have been surprised. In mid-1956, after Egypt's dictator, Gamal Abdal Nasser, turned his country sharply to the left, the United States canceled a grant to help build the Aswan High Dam. Nasser promptly nationalized the Suez Canal. Britain and France planned an invasion to restore international control, and Israel grabbed the moment to plan its own invasion of Egypt. Ike fumed in October 1956 when he learned of Israel's scheme to seize the Sinai. He protested, but the attack began on October 19. Next day came an Anglo-French ultimatum calling on both sides to pull back ten miles from the canal; Allied forces would move in to "guard it."

Things became extremely sticky when the USSR, on November 5, threatened to use force to restore peace. Ike, whose efforts to stop the conflict fizzled, also fumed at the Soviet threat and remarked that "if those fellows start something, we may have to hit 'em—and, if necessary, with everything in the bucket."

U.S. carriers and elements of the Sixth Fleet moved to evacuate Americans. Ike sent a clear message to the USSR by reinforcing the Mediterranean forces. Largely through the efforts of Lester Pearson, Canada's prime minister, the crisis cooled as UN peacekeepers intervened.

Ike pondered the multiple threats of communism, the Suez, and increasing demands for American soldiers around the globe. On January 5, 1957, he propounded the "Eisenhower Doctrine" as he asked Congress for authority to help a "nation or group of nations in the general area of the Middle East desiring . . . assistance."

Obviously military aid might be necessary—a further drain on the U.S. economy—but Congress in March approved. The president, under his doctrine, intervened in Jordan to preserve a Western-leaning monarch, again when Syria seemed toppling toward communism, and most forcefully in the Lebanon crisis of 1958 when he dispatched some 15,000 men to guarantee a free election to America's friends.

All these crises could not be met with massive retaliation; they proved the necessity for strong and flexible military options. They came at a crucial time for the U.S. Army, which had been floundering for a role in an atomic world.

Air defense artillery development, even missile development, seemed to nullify the army's usual role on a battlefield. What would an atomic battlefield be like? Where would the front be? Who could see what in the new clothing required? How supply the field forces? Some defense jugglers proposed a new "pentomic division" with five self-contained battle formations designed to operate independently in inconceivable chaos. This new division, though, proved unacceptable: strong in defense, it lacked offensive punch, and even nuclear wars relied on attack to win.

Ever since World War II scientists had become heavily involved in weapons development. American scientists had a long history of helping defend the nation—Lincoln helped sponsor the National Academy of Sciences in 1863 with a mandate to advise on scientific ways to help win the Civil War. Ordnance benefitted directly from scientific aid at the arsenals and proving grounds then and during the Spanish-

American War. In World War I, a combination of science, common sense, and factories helped improve planes from oddities to necessities. That combination increased as total war engulfed whole societies and fueled a frenzied march of technology. War's increasing sophistication welded civilian experts, scientists, and manufacturers together in a triumph of "weapons systems" over traditional arms. Such system developments as tactical nuclear devices, various toxic and tactical gases, chemical and biological warfare advances, and space age avionics and communications came from this fusion of brains and laboratories around the country.

Ike, in his farewell address, warned the nation against a "military-industrial complex" threatening democracy and a vigorous economy. That concern he bequeathed to his successor, John F. Kennedy, along with severed relations with Cuba and a half-baked CIA plan to aid some thirteen hundred Cuban exiles in a feeble invasion of Fidel Castro's Communist island. Leery about the whole operation, juggling concern about showing weakness versus problems in halting a near fait accompli, JFK unfortunately did not cancel the venture. He did brood that the lingering doctrine of massive retaliation might confound the outcome and lobbied for his own hope for the strategic possibilities of "flexible response."

In mid-April 1961 an intrepid thirteen hundred Cubans landed at the Bahia de los Cochinos (Bay of Pigs). Denied expected air support from a massed U.S. fleet nearby, the insurgents were swiftly overrun by 20,000 Castro militiamen. U.S. Secretary of the Navy John B. Connally and Chief of Naval Operations Arleigh Burke had anxiously waited for orders to send planes. But, as Connally recalled, "President Kennedy just would not do it. He was operating apparently under the illusion that nobody knew that the CIA was involved. And he didn't want to get publicly exposed as having supported this movement. . . . And so he wouldn't let us use . . . anything in support of the landing."[3] Air support might have ended Cuban communism. An alarmed Castro turned to the USSR for protection against Yankee aggression; his request offered a golden opportunity for Soviet expansion into the Western Hemisphere, and Nikita Khrushchev swiftly promised arms, an expeditionary army, and economic aid.

Kennedy learned from the Cuban fiasco. Accepting blame for it, he became personally involved and tougher in international relations. After a June 1961 confrontation with Khrushchev over the simmering issue of who controlled West Berlin, JFK ordered limited mobilization and won additional defense funds. His firm response avoided conflict but did result in the infamous Berlin Wall, built to stop emigration from East Berlin's dismal oppression. Nonetheless, the Soviet leader seemed determined to push JFK into mistakes of inexperience. Rumors began circulating in mid-1962 that Soviet bombers and medium-range ballistic missiles were in Cuba, weapons that threatened nuclear devastation to much of the Western Hemisphere.

The American president wanted conclusive proof and ordered satellite surveillance and increased spying on Cuba.

Proof came in mid-October 1962 that Soviet missile bases were being constructed in Cuba. Aware of a possible nuclear Armageddon, JFK held everything close to him, did not bring Congress into the fullness of coming disaster, and spent a nail-biting week in secret talks with a group called the ExComm (Executive Committee of the National Security Council). The president wanted the missiles gone; the question was, how? ExComm members proposed various solutions ranging from outright confrontation or a preemptive attack to diplomatic negotiations—none of which seemed either safe or sure. Finally the president demanded that the Soviets remove the missiles; threatened nuclear reprisals for any missiles used in the Americas; ordered planes, ships, and amphibious forces toward the Caribbean; and alerted the Strategic Air Command. With approval of the Organization of American States, he announced in late October a naval "quarantine" on weapons shipments to Cuba.

Both sides feared nuclear "accidents," and both jockeyed for something from the mess. A furious Khrushchev finally agreed to remove the missiles as JFK agreed to remove some old missiles from Turkey and made a public promise not to invade Cuba. By November the crisis ended. Khrushchev and JFK were criticized for being either too tough or too soft, but, in fact, they were careful to avoid war and used the crisis to improve relations. Results included a slowed nuclear arms race and the vital Limited Test Ban Treaty of 1963.

9

•

Vietnam

Another inheritance JFK received from Eisenhower was Vietnam. Ike inherited it from the French, whose old colonial claims were honored after World War II. Indochina, as Vietnam was known generally until the 1960s, still had lingering Gallic charms in some of its larger cities, especially Saigon, but public and political changes were menacingly deeper than the French realized. Japanese occupation quickened ancient seeds of nationalism. And from the war had come a Vietnamese hero—Ho Chi Minh.

As a staunch freedom fighter who had been helped by the U.S. Office of Strategic Services (forerunner of the CIA), Ho's migrations took him to China and to Moscow. He returned home a Communist with patriotic charisma.

France's return to Vietnam after World War II met surprising resistance. Ho declaimed against it, and a sullen rebellion sputtered, its roots apparently in Ho's city of Hanoi. As more French troops arrived to pacify the colony, rebel forces, called the Vietminh, attacked French outposts and columns in a widening guerrilla conflict. In 1954, after a disastrous loss at the Battle of Dien Bien Phu, France admitted defeat, and in 1955 left a Vietnam divided by international agreement, with a democratic republic in the South and Ho's Communist republic in the North.

Ike had sent supplies, equipment, and a few "advisers" to the French, but he shied away from direct intervention. Limited aid had expanded, and President Kennedy found a good number of U.S. advisers in a South Vietnam sorely threatened by an aggressive North and by serious internal problems. JFK, hewing to the Truman Doctrine, decided that communism's spread in Asia had to be stopped, and Vietnam looked like the place of best resistance. By 1962 more than 11,000 U.S. advisers were there. Deeply worried as the South grew weaker, and infuriated at covert U.S. conniving in assassinating the South's autocratic president, Ngo Dinh Diem, on November 1, 1963, JFK probed for new directions in the Far East. Suddenly, on November 22, he, too, was assassinated.

Lyndon B. Johnson now inherited Vietnam. As vice president LBJ had visited Saigon, seen the kind of incipient chaos that touched most of the South, and concluded that President Diem alone could hold things together. He guessed correctly that a competent successor would be hard to find. He also guessed that the U.S. mission in Saigon was too involved in Vietnam's daily doings and distrusted the ambassador, Henry Cabot Lodge. Lodge proceeded to involve himself in finding a new president for South Vietnam and soon opened a revolving door to a sad list of generals lacking political or strategic sense. Diem's efforts at improving the army and stabilizing the economy disintegrated in a wash of graft, indolence, and stupidity.

Devoted to the Great Society—a vast plan of domestic reforms—LBJ tried to avoid foreign entanglement by following JFK's Vietnam plans. What were they? Did the late president plan to get out or get further in? Did his personal emphasis on Special Forces (Green Berets) suggest a hit-and-run strategy? No real answers came to these questions. JFK's cabinet argued over what he intended; some said he was going to pull out, others that the sending of more advisers showed he was going in—and a historical debate still rages!

Johnson, juggling fears about South Vietnam's survival against the Truman Doctrine, sought input from Saigon, Paris, and London, and from Washington itself. The French opposed deeper involvement, the British were ambivalent, and Washington wallowed.

LBJ moved cautiously, trying to save South Vietnam without getting sucked into a sinkhole that might derail his Great Society campaign. As he pushed his economic, social, and civil rights programs, he cocked an eye toward Vietnam—where continuing political incoherence frazzled military operations and North Vietnam openly sent massive supplies and troops to its Viet Cong (Communist) puppets in the South. LBJ appointed Gen. William C. Westmoreland to replace the Commander, U.S. Military Assistance Command, Vietnam (COMUSMACV), and sent Gen. Maxwell Taylor to replace Ambassador Henry Cabot Lodge.

Energetic, innovative, and fresh on the scene, both generals carried LBJ's high hopes and confidence. The continuing political instability sapped the morale of the Army of the Republic of Vietnam (ARVN) and spread a resigned kind of torpor through the countryside. Defeats dogged the ARVN throughout 1964, and General Westmoreland called for more troops to save the South. LBJ complied, and by the end of 1964 some 23,000 U.S. advisers were closely coordinating ARVN actions. LBJ noted the few words of caution from some advisers but sent in more men.

Early Sunday morning, August 2, 1964, a shocked president learned about a North Vietnamese torpedo boat attack on the U.S. destroyer *Maddox* in the Tonkin Gulf off North Vietnam's coast. True, *Maddox* was covertly collecting electronic intelligence for South Vietnam, but it had been safely beyond territorial limits. *Maddox* took one hit and sped out of range. Two days later insubstantial reports of an attack on another destroyer added to the confusion. LBJ ordered a retaliatory bombing raid on a North Vietnamese navy base on August 5, and two days later he won overwhelming congressional support for the Tonkin Gulf Resolution, which gave him wide discretionary authority to "take all necessary steps, including the use of armed forces," to repel attacks or help Communist-threatened Asian nations.

Although severely criticized later for sneaking the resolution past Congress, Johnson carefully discussed it with congressional leaders the evening of August 4. He won their full support, and on August 7 the resolution passed nearly unanimously. At the time neither he nor his close advisers wanted an expanded conflict—he held the resolution as a hole card as he pondered how much U.S. assistance was enough. The resolution might intimidate the North Vietnamese and invigorate southerners.

Johnson, increasingly irked by North Vietnamese Army (NVA) incursions via what was known as the Ho Chi Minh Trail along the Laotian and Cambodian borders, pushed a bombing program in the North that spawned more enemies than it killed. Shocked that each U.S. troop increase was outmatched by the enemy, Military Assistance Command, Vietnam (MACV) finally suggested that the Allies had grossly underestimated North Vietnam's dedication to winning. LBJ expanded the war by sending MACV fighting reinforcements.

Canny Gen. Vo Nguyen Giap, NVA leader and victor of Dien Bien Phu, reorganized and rearmed VC (Viet Cong) units and spread the tactics of "people's war." By 1965 rumor had it that the days belonged to the ARVN

President Lyndon Johnson (far left corner) greeting U.S. troops in Vietnam, 1966. Courtesy of National Archives.

and their Yank collaborators, while nights belonged to the VC. The night frights did serious damage to civilian morale and to ARVN control of villages and districts. Black-clad VC prowled as patriots; they demanded food, money, and recruits, killed and burned, and often joined the ARVN with daylight.

Guerrilla war was not unknown to Americans; Indians and Filipinos were efficient teachers. But lessons were lost in the whelm of great wars and massive forces. MACV had everything handy to win a big, open war with the NVA, but American troops—except the Special Forces—were not trained for night stalking, jungle patrolling, political assassinations—things somehow passé, certainly un-American. A few World War II veterans of Pacific island-hopping were ripe with blooded wisdom but were hardly heard.

MACV focused too long on forcing the enemy into major battles; when they did not happen, U.S. and ARVN units tried a limited application of Westmoreland's search-and-destroy strategy, but when night fell they holed up in fire bases, stayed close to artillery support, and yielded too much countryside.

A stream of "fact finders" from the White House reported back that things were improving by late 1965—more men would win it. How many more?, the president pondered. For how long? But he complied, and by mid-1965 more than 200,000 U.S. troops were fighting in Vietnam.

As the southern government stabilized finally, Johnson began pushing that "other war," a campaign to win massive popular support in South Vietnam by active relief, medical and educational, and self-defense efforts. LBJ sent Robert Komer to head a huge pacification program aimed at winning "hearts and minds." Tough, realistic, and armed with clout, Komer developed an effort to reach down to villages and encourage loyalty to South Vietnam. A good idea proved hard to effect since local loyalty flexed with night and day. He boasted early success; but when, at last, his counterinsurgency lagged, the CIA began the Phoenix program—a scheme to coordinate results from myriad intelligence sources, identify leading Viet Cong in villages and districts, and arrest or kill them. Brutal—appalling, some said—but Phoenix, according to NVA sources, proved the most debilitating enemy they faced during the war.

With soldiers going almost daily to Asia-bound ships, with the ARVN leaving most combat now to the Yankees, LBJ's frustration became a kind of fixed desperation. Vietnam absorbed most of his time by 1967. His cherished Great Society floundering in the wake of an escalating war budget, his defense advisers bereft of plans to win, he himself bashed by the press about a "credibility gap" between what he said and did, Johnson wondered, "What the hell can I do?" Cabinet members faced increasingly skeptical congressional committees with questions about men, money, and success. Vietnam shimmered as a kind of reverse virtual reality where plans sloughed to wistful wishes and farce reigned supreme. It especially galled LBJ because his 1965 effort to save the Dominican Republic from disaster had been a near showcase of efficient success. Why the difference? Probably because the Dominican crisis came on his watch, he held all the tokens of power in his hands, and had no worries of Armageddon.

Vietnam could well bring Armageddon, which is why the commander-in-chief frugally doled men to Westmoreland, restricted ground operations to South Vietnam itself, and denied access to enemy supply routes in Laos and Cambodia.

Wars have ways of setting their own course, hence confusing both mice and men. Vietnam set contradictory courses that confused even Pentagon gurus. So many new weapons seemed to negate the need for strategy, and firepower would replace tactics. Casualties, an American anathema, would likely be mostly due to accidents. Helicopters equipped with Puff the Magic Dragon (an ultra high-speed machine gun) could engorge whole acres with lead; helicopters later, too, could defoliate whole jungles with

Agent Orange and debilitate humans in a lingering toxicity. And all of this was true and false.

Casualties proved illusory at best. MACV's daily "body counts" were thin while endless lines of body bags trooped nightly across world television screens like a ghostly accusation. LBJ suffered them personally, read their names with breakfast, and tried to writhe the horror to an end. Anguish led him to a natural but serious mistake—he micromanaged the war, especially the air war. Daily lists came from the White House on targets for the day, targets that often irked fliers for their triviality and for avoiding the big North Vietnamese port of Haiphong. LBJ feared that smashing that port would bring the Soviet Union and China into the war. He did, however, so often target Hanoi that it developed at last the most modern, most deadly antiaircraft system in the world. Missions there were nearly suicidal or sent survivors to the inhumanity of cells in the "Hanoi Hilton." Prison atrocities escalated on both sides.

High-tech victory loomed another illusion. Although U.S. mobility, artillery, firepower, and light artillery dominated roads and Landing Zones (LZ), and high-level bombing by B-52s did surprising damage, the VC's AK-47 rifles, their mortars and grenade launchers, their pungee sticks in rice paddies, and their wily jungle snares seemed oddly to even the odds. True, too, even in the war in the Mekong Delta where ambushes, traps, and mines taught new lessons in riverine combat.

Everything about the U.S.-Vietnam situation wobbled in uncertainty. By November 1965 Secretary of Defense Robert McNamara's enthusiasm dwindled and his reports shifted from victory to saving South Vietnam to hopes of hanging on. Westmoreland kept asking for men; he remained certain that numbers would prevail. Alone with his conscience at night, the president grappled with sending more men after dead ones or simply failing out of the war. Determined not to be the first American president to lose a war (he forgot Jefferson Davis), he could not quit. But his frequent peace feelers failed; the enemy numbers increased; there were almost 400,000 GIs in Vietnam, along with a good many Allied forces, especially from South Korea and Australia, yet there came no victory.

In January 1967 Westmoreland began an offensive to win the war. Putting the ARVN in charge of rear area security and pacification, he committed 30,000 of his 450,000 troops to an attack some forty miles north of Saigon against a huge VC staging area called the Iron Triangle and kept going. Heavy fighting continued in a series of operations from February through April. Striking hard at the Central Highlands, GIs won a major battle at Dak To in November. On a crest, LBJ allowed a number of free-fire zones that permitted B-52 carpet bombing, artillery barrages, and defoliation. MACV dramatically announced that a crossover point had come and that the enemy were now losing more than they could replace. There would be more fighting, but there would be victory.

With NVA reinforcements trickling in, the war slogged into a kind of stalemate. American news media reflected Westmoreland's optimism. TV poses of power flowed from U.S. air bases, fire bases, and GIs. There were doomsayers, though, who doubted the good statistics from MACV or the effectiveness of pacification.

On January 30, 1968, South Vietnam exploded under a series of VC attacks coinciding with a cynically violated Tet holiday. Coordinated attacks against cities and military bases were expected to trigger a great popular southern uprising against the Yankee occupation.

A direct assault on the U.S. Embassy in Saigon ran in full color across the evening TV news. Several defenders held the buildings, but scenes of VC rushing the grounds in a mini-firefight shocked Americans—especially since the government boasted quick victory. Tet proved a dismal failure for the VC. They lost some 50,000 men, so many that NVA troops were rushed to save what was left. ARVN and U.S. forces clearly won the battle, but losses were heavy.

Truth is always a war casualty. With screens continually filled with havoc, the American public lost faith in victory. College campuses spawned teach-ins as a huge antiwar movement nearly destabilized the country.

Most disillusioned of all was LBJ. He had watched Tet and the coincidental siege of a mountainous fortress called Khe Sanh and appreciated final successes there; but his political savvy told him the people no longer supported the war. He replaced Westmoreland with Gen. Creighton Abrams, who fought aggressively but promised no quick victory. Personally crushed and concerned for the body politic, Johnson sought peace and mollification of internal strife by announcing his decision not to run again for the presidency.

Peace talks began in May 1968, but there came no peace. While casualties piled up, Richard Nixon became president in 1969. Nervous about Soviet plans for Europe, Nixon worked on détente; seizing on global worries about chemical and biological warfare, he unilaterally stopped U.S. research in these areas and destroyed existing stockpiles—actions that finally produced a treaty banning such weapons.

One of Nixon's boasts during his election campaign had been that he had a plan for getting out of Vietnam. He had one, a novel one—widen the war and let the enemy think him a loose cannon that might do anything, including atom bombing North Vietnam. Not only did he continue the fighting, he expanded its limits to Cambodia in April 1970 and to Laos in February 1971 in attempts to cut the supply chain from Hanoi to the South.

These ventures had some success, especially in encouraging the ARVN, but they met brutal resistance at home; antiwar rallies nearly became wars themselves. Nixon, undeterred, then actively pushed the program of "Vietnamization" to upgrade the training and arming of the ARVN, which would allow U.S. withdrawal from Vietnam. The president did promise air support if the North attacked again. He also allowed the mining of Haiphong harbor. A cease-fire came in October 1971, but trouble continued, and U.S. planes saved the South from an invasion in 1972. By April 1973, U.S. troops all were home.

By then, though, the president's attention reverted to his main concern for European détente with a decided loss of interest in the Far East. His concern centered, too, on his own Watergate problems, which led him to resign. When another NVA invasion came in March 1975, President Gerald Ford could not muster congressional support for ARVN air cover, and in April 1975 South Vietnam collapsed. More than 58,000 Americans had died trying to save it, and most survivors returned to a resentful welcome from a disunited nation.

Angered by what it saw as presidents warring around it, in November 1973 a war-weary and disillusioned Congress passed the War Powers Resolution, designed to limit presidential authority to send U.S. forces into action without congressional approval—basically a reminder of a constitutional prerogative. Hotly disputed by future chief executives, the resolution is honored mostly by circumvention.

"In Our Day Wars Are Not Won by Mere Enthusiasm, but by Technical Superiority."

—V. I. Lenin, 1918

Vietnam taught a good many military lessons, most of which were hastily dustbinned in a shame of losing what had seemed an unlosable war. JFK's favorite Special Forces appeared less useful than predicted, their covert actions conveniently suppressed. Fire bases and strong points were out of vogue; old truths about objective, initiative, clear chains of command, and adaptive tactics were whitewashed in the excuse of fighting with weak, indecisive allies unable to make a country.

Some U.S. advantages persisted: superior logistical and medical capabilities; highly developed air mobility as the helicopter came into its own; new, effective riverine operations by the "brown water navy" in the Mekong Delta. The nimble fire support from the air force to the infantry would be further refined.

Even if Vietnam was lost, there would clearly be other conflicts. What would these conflicts involve? The whole military structure of the nation, from the president to the Pentagon, to the gobs, grunts, and airmen, would have to be recast according to models, myths, and maybes. After Vietnam, American ways of fighting changed.

In any military time of troubles there is a natural urge to get back to basics, to do what used to work. Kipling put it fairly clearly in "The Young British Soldier":

> If your officer's dead and the sergeants look white,
> Remember it's ruin to run from a fight:
> So take open order, lie down and sit tight,
> And wait for supports like a soldier.

And supports were coming, precedents that suddenly became once more the essential things to do: get ready for the war that was likely to be fought in Europe, the war the services had expected for years. It would be what was somehow called a conventional war, one involving vast armies, tanks, planes, artillery, perhaps even battles using tactical nukes. High-level thinking turned back to NATO; presidents agreed and the Pentagon modeled; the CIA turned to known ways of spying; the navy built carriers and nuclear subs, and all came right in martial matters.

Luck and some miscalculation made possible the return to an old future: luck because during the Vietnam diversion, the Soviets did not move west; miscalculation because they were still too weak to strike NATO. True, large Red armies existed, Red fleets burgeoned, and the Red air force sported some of the fastest, toughest military aircraft, with bombers capable of delivering many of their atom bombs. Weaknesses, though, lurked in their unstable politics, their command rigidity, their ponderous logistical and procurement infrastructure, and their errors about NATO's strength.

Peace persisted because of Mutual Assured Destruction (MAD), bomb versus bomb. In a defensive mode after Vietnam, the United States and its allies once more hunched behind the Bomb, and so did the Soviets. Unreasonable, yes; unthinkable, no; and mutual terror did create a bizarre sort of escalating one-upmanship that pitted words in the UN and promoted a game of chicken between U.S. and Soviet submarines, ships, and outposts. China got into the act as its own forces grew and its craving for Taiwan sent an American fleet to temper any "adventurism."

Fortunately, not all of the army's thinkers were numbed by the "Vietnam syndrome" or by a decade's advance to the past. Long experience with varied peacekeeping and policing activities led the U.S. Marines to publish *The Small Wars Manual* in the 1930s and to revise it in 2004. Marines still rely on much of the philosophy and strategy the book offers.

For the United States, said the manual, "small wars are operations undertaken under executive authority" to apply armed force and diplomacy "in the internal or external affairs of another state whose government is unstable, inadequate for the preservation of life," and obstructive to U.S. foreign policy. Large wars aim at total victory. "This is seldom true in small wars," where objectives waver between such military and civil functions as suppressing (or encouraging) revolt while policing the streets and protecting everyday life. In the years after Vietnam, small wars would bulk large in U.S. affairs.

Much Pentagon time still went to preparing for "conventional" war, while a sea change in public thinking forced new emphases on high-tech weapons—missiles; tactical nukes; stronger, faster multipurpose aircraft armed with long-distance weapons and fortified by nearly magical optics for offense and defense; self-contained naval battle groups built around modern carriers to project American power wherever needed. Public acceptance came easily to a nation tired of war and grimly opposed to casualties—these deadly new toys would save lives and make the United States invulnerable!

10

•

The Cold War

Certainly the globe's defining confrontation during the last half of the twentieth century, the Cold War had few cool moments, either factually or metaphorically. The name covers a congeries of struggles—economic, emotional, diplomatic, military, psychological, sometimes farcical—between democracy and dictatorship. In the sense that the Cold War focused the energies and genius of capitalism and communism, it became an apocalyptic constant like the conflicts in George Orwell's *1984*.

Historians argue still about when and how the Cold War started, and about who started it. A commonly accepted view is that seeds were planted at the Potsdam Conference in 1945 and sprouted with Churchill's "Iron Curtain" speech, but some argue that a kind of rabid anti-Bolshevism infected America far earlier and conditioned relations with Russia before World War I. Bolsheviks were revolutionaries against capitalistic regimes they wanted replaced by a victorious proletariat. The general idea appealed to American liberal groups such as labor unions. Out of the struggle of workers against managers came a deep-struck American fear of an anticapitalist revolution that might follow Russia's march to radical socialism. When Woodrow Wilson became president, the nation wallowed in a kind of autarkic hubris.

Neither autarkist nor autocrat, Wilson saw his own fears grow during

World War I as soviets (self-elected councils of mutinous soldiers) almost wrecked the French Army and infected Gallic politics. When the czarist regime collapsed in the 1917 revolution between Lenin's Reds and the nationalistic Whites, Wilson reluctantly joined Allied efforts to topple the tottering Reds. His indecision about what to do only confused the issue, and communism won. Shortly after the Great War, America succumbed to a numbing Red Scare that led to a shameful erosion of civil rights under the rubric of preserving the national interest.

Great Britain, too, shied away from Russia, and that troubled country soon found itself isolated and boycotted by expanding Western anticommunism. Mutual distrust escalated as the emerging Union of Soviet Socialist Republics turned inward and began building a self-reliant "great socialist state." When Joseph Stalin became leader, the USSR spurned the West—save once, when it tried to help the Nationalists in the Spanish Civil War, which increased Western anger because the Nationalists were considered Communists.

Even Lend-Lease and the Second Front of World War II hardly dimmed Soviet suspicion of Allied perfidy, suspicion the Potsdam Conference only deepened. Bitter realization that Stalin would resist relinquishing even a yard of conquered territories turned the Allies to Truman's containment programs, which included the Marshall Plan (a program that deserves to share the praise Churchill awarded Lend-Lease, the "most unsordid act in history"), and which did help sustain democracy in Greece, Turkey, and Italy. Truman's actions may well mark the real start of the conflict.

In the late 1940s the Cold War bubbled toward boiling as one crisis followed another. In June 1948 the Soviets blockaded road and rail lines through their zone of occupation in an effort to force the Americans, British, and French out of Berlin. This blockade triggered the herculean Allied airlift, which, combined with a counter-blockade of goods going to the Soviet sector, pushed Stalin into reopening Berlin the following May. Further pressured by NATO's creation in April 1949, the USSR retaliated late that summer by exploding a nuclear bomb over Siberia. Mao Zedong defeated what was left of Chiang Kai-shek's Nationalists—they withdrew to Taiwan (Formosa) in December—and spread communism fully over mainland China. These examples of Sino-Soviet expansionism pushed President Truman's new Department of Defense and National Security Council to urge massive U.S. rearmament and a hard line against continuing Communist aggrandizement.

A Red Scare reminiscent of the one after the Great War smothered the United States in fears of Communist conspiracies. Soviet spying added supposed fact to fancy. In America anticommunism became anti-Sovietism and inspired demagogues like Senator Joseph McCarthy of Wisconsin, who spouted specious charges against hundreds and ruined lives by innuendo. Fellow senators were slow to condemn a man they feared might turn on them. Truman succumbed and demanded loyalty oaths from federal employees; leftist organizations were hounded, even unions; conformity smothered personal liberties as all deviants from God-fearing democracy were damned; homosexuals (known as "pinko queers"), writers, actors, artists, and teachers were held hostage to suspicion. A cowed public adjusted to thought control, although dissension rumbled. McCarthyism spread until the mid-1950s when the civil rights movement chafed the conscience of a beleaguered democracy and America broke free again.

Dwight Eisenhower replaced Truman; American defense policy shifted and embraced MAD to assure containment. Nikita Khrushchev, Stalin's successor in 1953, hewed still to global competition and used the power of the new Warsaw Pact nations to crush a Hungarian rebellion in 1956—an action that unsettled the pact. By the late 1980s members drifted off to indifference or independence. Growing caution after the Cuban Missile Crisis led to mutual awareness of peace or annihilation; the Limited Test Ban Treaty of 1963 marked the first cooling of the war.

Sudden distractions diverted the attentions of East and West. While the United States struggled in Vietnam, and the USSR sank into a bitter feud with Red China, coexistence held uneasy sway.

As appetites for power went unsatisfied, a rapprochement between the United States and China, engineered by George H.W. Bush, Henry Kissinger, and President Nixon in 1972, scared the Soviets enough to bring about the first SALT (Strategic Arms Limitation Talks) agreement, which limited deployment of antiballistic missiles and restricted offensive nuclear missiles. Another SALT agreement in 1974 pushed both sides further from brinkmanship. An uneasy accommodation continued until December 1979, when the Soviets invaded Afghanistan to save a decaying Communist government.

Jimmy Carter, becoming president of the United States in 1977, determined to focus on peace and human rights. But Soviet aggressiveness, not only in Afghanistan but also in Cuba, dimmed his hopes. Dogged by ill luck, Carter's diplomatic successes were tarnished by wobbling will. Commendable moral grounds led him to prod the United States to return the canal to Panama—which made him a wimp to many Americans. His normalization of Chinese relations and adroit conjuring of peace between Israel and Egypt in 1978 were overshadowed when the staff of the U.S.

Embassy in Teheran were taken hostage in 1979. Failed diplomatic and economic sanctions designed to force Iran to free the hostages led to a seriocomic rescue fiasco that made both president and country look silly. Disheartened, Carter finally endorsed much more money for defense, restored draft registration, and approved a rapid deployment force. In 1980 he proclaimed the Carter Doctrine, extending containment to the Persian Gulf area.

Ronald Reagan, a successful Hollywood actor and former governor of California, breezed into the White House in 1981 with ample confidence, charm, and popularity to sustain big changes—though his boldness struck some as Hollywood swashbuckling. Inheriting a slowing economy, hectic unemployment, labor unrest, and much diplomatic disdain, Reagan began cleaning house. Old doctrines were archived, all policies reexamined as America's future shifted. Although he was no dummy by most measures, the president's limited economic knowledge did expose him to self-anointed experts who told him what he wanted to hear about tax cutting as the sure way to prosperity. Supply-side economists—nonmainstream ones, that is—argued an idyllic cycle in which tax cuts would stimulate production and business expansion, hence creating jobs and increasing the tax base, which, in turn, would stimulate spending, which would create more production, more jobs, and higher exports. Assumptions being uncertain, the economy first sagged into a major recession by 1982 and revived slowly.

It revived really because of Reagan's basic ignorance of diplomacy, an ignorance that permitted him to believe in a world without either the USSR or communism itself. That led him to a major shift in American foreign policy, a shift reinforced by his supply-side thinking, which negated public parsimony. A proud patriot who detested communism, Reagan soon scrapped the notion of containing the USSR and began a general offensive.

Containment may have worked but was no longer necessary; the time had come to take back some areas stolen by the Soviets. Confrontation replaced coexistence. A bit skeptical at first, the public came to enjoy the president's amiable truculence as he pushed hard against what he called "the Evil Empire." He and Caspar Weinberger, his secretary of defense, launched the most relentless military buildup in peacetime America at a decade's cost of some $2.4 trillion. Reagan had several purposes behind his saber-smithing. First, he wanted American might to halt Soviet greed; second, he wanted to stimulate the economy; third, he urged development of new weapons and weapons systems—missiles, myriad warships, planes, tanks—as a way to overreach Soviet technology. More than that, he proposed a technologically risky Strategic Defense Initiative—popularly called Star Wars—not only to suppress a missile attack but also to escalate the arms race beyond Soviet resources. Chilly reality stalked the Kremlin. The government paper *Izvestia* moaned that Americans "want to impose on us an even more ruinous arms race," and General Secretary Yuri Andropov saw Star Wars as "a bid to disarm the Soviet Union." Andrei Gromyko, veteran diplomat, understood that "behind all this lies the clear calculation that the USSR will exhaust its material resources . . . and therefore will be forced to surrender."[1]

In addition Reagan announced a doctrine of support for anti-Soviet fighters anywhere. Covert CIA help in Central America, Africa, and the Middle East, as well as nearly overt aid to anti-Communists in Afghanistan, strained diplomatic and legal boundaries—but strained the Soviets fiercely. An expedition to help Christian militia in Lebanon ended in disaster when a truck bomb killed 231 U.S. Marines and others on October 23, 1983. Reagan pulled the Marines out, but two days later he approved an invasion of Grenada, a small Caribbean nation, without troubling congressional consciences.

Grenada lingers as a special case in Reagan's militancy. Although he gets blamed for the venture, Reagan actually responded to a request from Prime Minister Mary Eugenia Charles of Dominica, who headed the Organization of the Eastern Caribbean States, to save their member island, Grenada, from a vicious Communist regime with close ties to Cuba. Her plea fitted the Reagan Doctrine neatly—as well as the old Monroe Doctrine. It also flew in the face of the Brezhnev Doctrine that no Communist ground would be lost to capitalism.

Her plea also might confirm the Weinberger and Powell doctrines. In 1984 Weinberger publicly stated that the United States should commit forces only where national interests were at stake and then do so with clear objectives, sufficient forces to meet those objectives, the intention of winning, and the reasonable assurance of congressional and public support. Reflecting his experiences in Vietnam, Powell also believed that America should never go to war except to protect clearly endangered national interests, and then only with strong public support, overwhelming force, and a clearly defined exit strategy. With some warping of these principles, Urgent Fury began October 25, 1983, when some twelve hundred Army Rangers and Marines arrived in Grenada and met surprising resistance. Reinforcements brought U.S. numbers up to some seven thousand, and, finally, they ousted the Red government and arranged democratic elections. Urgent Fury ranks a frazzled example of a campaign arranged so hastily that troops

President Ronald Reagan walking with Prime Minister Margaret Thatcher of Great Britain, Camp David, 1986. A staunch ally and fellow Cold Warrior, the Baroness Thatcher in her June 2004 eulogy to her friend and colleague said, "The world mourns the passing of the Great Liberator and echoes his prayer 'God Bless America.' " Courtesy of Ronald Reagan Presidential Library.

lacked such basics as maps, secure communications, clear objectives—or enough of anything!

Reagan's anti-Soviet zeal sometimes exceeded his wisdom. Some of the CIA's covert meddlings were examples of too much presidential ardor; but Nicaragua ranks as the worst both for carnage and for backlash.

Americans had long meddled in Nicaragua and considered its location vital to Yankee security. Virtual civil war reigned by the 1970s as Anastasio Somoza's brutal dictatorship spawned a new wave of rebels sustained by President Carter's campaign for human rights. In 1979, leftist rebels calling themselves Sandinistas—a touchstone to a longtime national hero—chucked out the fascist Somoza regime and began their own dictatorship, which engendered another rebellion. Reagan, true to his doctrine, determined to help the Nicaraguan "Contras" as well as other anti-Communists trying to hold on to El Salvador. Congress forbade direct aid to the Contras. Reagan then finagled money for them by secret and illegal arms sales to Iran. The Iran-Contra affair nearly ruined Reagan.

But in 1988, when he and General Secretary Mikhail Gorbachev signed the INF (Intermediate Range Nuclear Forces) Treaty, which destroyed all short- and intermediate range missiles, Reagan's stock zoomed. This marked the first time that the United States and the Soviets had agreed to eliminate any strategic weapons. The impulse really came from Gorbachev, whose rise to power in Moscow surprised old-line Communists. In March 1985, this new General Secretary of the Communist Party announced, "We can't go on living like this." Soon he stunned the USSR and the world with reforms he hoped would save the nation, but their depth and scope unhinged what was left of the economy and replaced tyranny with freedom.

So came the beginning of the end. There would be skirmishes as Gorbachev pressed reforms, but the USSR finally went broke in mind and money, disintegrated, and lost the Cold War.

Some historians argue that the USSR really collapsed from internal failure. Others cite earlier presidents' contributions and the fact that Congress supported Reagan's relentless offensive that bankrupted the entire Soviet system. Still others give much credit to Gorbachev's boldness. Two witnesses should be heard on the issue. Henry Kissinger thought that Reagan's vision, toughness, patience, and flexibility produced "the most stunning diplomatic feat of the modern era." Margaret Thatcher, no mean Cold Warrior herself, said that "Reagan won the cold war without firing a shot."[2]

"What a Beautiful Fix We Are in Now: Peace Has Been Declared."
—Napoleon I, after the Treaty of Amiens, 1802

In a way the whole thing seemed somehow inglorious. There were no titanic battles, no big bang—the enemy just sort of seeped away and left an almost wistful void. In the wake of the USSR's dissolution, the United States floundered, out of focus, without communism and without a daily threat of Armageddon. There were a few problems remindful of the end of World War II—caught on a crest of rearming, America's economy slowed. But a jubilantly expected "peace dividend" would fix that and get the country back to business. Though the dividend looked more like a market blip, isolationism, a normal peacetime bane, did not return because the world as marketplace refocused America's energies.

Problems like the national debt, trade imbalances, GNP could be handled by a world appetite for all things American. And, be it said for the Cold War, its necessities had indeed bred advances in medicine, metallurgy, transportation, TV, wireless and satellite technology, espionage, and entertainment. Soviet competition spurred not only American space ventures, but an array of military inventions: accurate target acquisition computers for artillery; more mobile big guns; "smart bomb" guided missiles on land, sea, and air; unmanned cruise missiles; Kevlar and its various uses from body armor to helmets; night vision goggles that brought light to dark fighting; multipurpose mines; vastly improved infantry rifles and grenades; new, lighter, more lethal machine guns; a whole new breed of techno-sciences that revolutionized aircraft and tank design and produced antimetallic smokes; as well as biological and chemical warfare personnel protection; rapid antimissile Aegis systems for naval warfare; partially ceramic nuclear submarines; vastly improved communications; and near magical medical support systems. All of these came from America's huge industrial capacity, which depended on new management techniques.

So the United States had lots to sell, especially with the expected military shrinkage. With such a modern arsenal, a large peacetime military establishment made small sense. Now wars could be waged and won with nearly bloodless frugality, as Reagan's small campaigns seemed to affirm. The new enginery of war would make casualties insignificant. This attitude turned the United States from hostility to the international arms trade into the world's largest "merchant of death." Many World War II and Korean era weapons went on the market—which might not have been all bad had the sales been shaped to aid and influence pro-American countries. Dumped on the world through official and covert CIA channels, these arms—plus those of the defunct USSR—brought new and nearly global terrorism.

Some American institutions were left adrift. For a good many abroad, the CIA, a Cold War institution spawned under the National Security Act of 1947, seemed a terrorist organization. In the 1950s "the Company," as it was quixotically called, expanded its undercover operations far beyond mere intelligence gathering. With presidential encouragement, funded from secret budgets, operating almost without tether, the agency pursued psychological and political warfare as its agents financed, supplied, and trained guerrillas for some anti-Communist regimes and abetted unrest for others—witness Iran (1953) and Guatemala (1954). Often buffeted by public and congressional suspicion and wobbling efforts at oversight, the Directors of Central Intelligence (DCIs) altered policies according to politics. Covert operations alternated with traditional human spying (HUMINT) and high-altitude photographic surveillance (IMINT), often with vital results. Information from a Moscow officer turned American spy and also from photo analysis revealed the Soviet nuclear missiles installed in Cuba, which brought a U.S. victory in the Cold War.

Covert action escalated during the Vietnam War as the CIA ran what amounted to a secret war of terror and counterintelligence—which backfired in MACV (Military Assistance Command, Vietnam), presidential, and public resentment. While the Company made some of its troubles, a basic American distrust of "dirty tricks," assassination attempts, and even reading other people's mail frustrated much of its effort. Sometimes ordered into such illegal activities as Operation Chaos (snooping on domestic opponents of the Vietnam War), the agency came under fierce congressional investigation and reform.

President Reagan grabbed the agency with gusto, revitalized it, and aimed it back to covert activities—witness Afghanistan, Angola, and Nicaragua. The Intelligence Reform Act of 1980 opened new channels for the agency; new tools were available, such as SIGINT (satellite and signals communications) and increased cooperation with military intelligence units—especially with the navy's submarine and seabed acoustics people. But some internal scandals (discovery of two longtime Soviet moles high in the agency) and the end of the Cold War blurred the Company's future.

Unexpected peace spawns some inconveniences. The USSR's disintegration deranged not only the CIA but also the U.S. Army. Without a looming big war, what mission did a land force have? Obviously the navy and air force would have roles in maintaining the coming Pax Americana, but the army? Military theorists proposed drastic reductions in force, the creation of a sort of international police arm to support air and sea power. Army brass sought niches in missile defense and occupation roles, but continued weapons research and development.

Perspective on the Cold War is elusive. It centered American presidents in the international arena. More than that, it provided the comfort of a recognized evil so that virtually everything could fit under the rubric of anticommunism—from Truman's containment doctrine (including Korea and Vietnam) to resurgent American imperialism under Reagan, McCarthyism, the arms race, the politicizing of American media, and new tools of slaughter.

Additionally, the Cold War underscored the importance of the UN as that organization took more responsibility for peacekeeping missions around the globe—albeit not always with the wholehearted approval of the United States! Sovereignty remained the big problem with U.S. and UN relations—although future concerns of collective security trimmed some American suspicions. Yielding any power over U.S. interests to anything out of the country never sits well with U.S. administrations—especially yielding military command to other nations. An irksome rumor persists that American troops have never been commanded by foreign officers, despite the facts of World War I and II, plus lesser ventures in the policing business.

An almost predictable leftover of the frigid conflict: rising nationalism around the world. Perhaps its most terrible legacy is damage to the Western democratic spirit.

.

11

———————— • ————————

New War, Old Cost

"The pursuit of victory without slaughter is likely to lead to slaughter without victory."

—John Churchill, First Duke of Marlborough (1650–1722)

Like Ronald Reagan, his successor in the White House was no pushover. George Herbert Walker Bush's experience as a navy combat flier and as Reagan's vice president, his diplomatic service in China, his stint as CIA director, and his time in Congress served him well in the presidency. Uncertain in domestic matters, he was sure-footed and innovative in foreign affairs—an invaluable asset to a chief executive involved in tidying up the Cold War and finishing off the Evil Empire.

Bush inherited not only Reagan's ideas and programs, but also a good many unresolved problems—most of them diplomatic. First in line, of course, were happenings in the fragmenting USSR. Reagan had not only urged the Evil Empire to self-implosion, he had it well on the skids when Bush took over. The new administration found that the skids lacked grease and the slide was going to be rough. Mikhail Gorbachev's swaying leadership complicated his own problems as such satellite states as Latvia, Lithuania, Estonia, Belorussia, Azerbaijan, Armenia, and even Georgia and the

President George H. W. Bush and President Mikhail Gorbachev signing the Strategic Arms Reduction Treaty (START) at the Kremlin, Moscow, July 31, 1991. Courtesy of George Bush Presidential Library.

Ukraine sprouted nationalistic organizations pushing for independence. As Bush well knew, crises are rarely singular. While Gorbachev struggled to stem secession and urge reform within the old USSR, his loosening grip on such westerly fiefdoms as the Baltic states, Poland, and Hungary had begun an unstoppable process.

A sea change swept Eastern Europe during the summer and fall of 1989. Polish workers shoved an eroded Soviet regime aside and surged to democracy. Hungary, a long-simmering problem, broke loose. Czechoslovakia began an autumn of liberation, and East Germany, that woefully drab satrapy led by a nearly fanatical Communist, watched its neighbors slough away and looked longingly at prosperity and freedom across the Wall. Gorbachev's earlier permissiveness created an insidiously Januslike problem for the West: as one order faded, how usher in a new one? The answer came almost obviously: unify Germany and realign the whole power structure in Europe.

Could Gorbachev tolerate this? After all, bifurcation and isolation of the Germans had been main Soviet policy since Stalin. Could France accept? A unified Germany raised old dreads among the French. Britain, Italy, Spain, Portugal, the Low Countries, and Scandinavia all had stakes in so radical a gamble. Gorbachev fiddled but finally agreed; so did all the others; and on November 9, 1989, one of the great haunts of the twentieth century—the Berlin Wall—crashed down, and all of Germany was free.

Final throes of the USSR sparked all kinds of dangers. Gorbachev staggered from openness (*glasnost*) to repression. President Bush, his foreign affairs team, and other Western leaders tried following Teddy Roosevelt's notion: "Tread softly and carry a big stick."

Before the Evil Empire did implode and go away, Gorbachev had been replaced by Boris Yeltsin, who inherited a shrunken nation in economic and social chaos, a people hoping that McDonald's, Coke signs, cars in the streets, Levi's, and tourists really were what they had waited, scrimped, and fought for—a tardy recompense for slavery.

No, the big stick proved not to be the Bomb, but freedom—a word whose power is too often ignored. Freedom to the Soviets was a magical concept of breath and breadth, of promise and reward, a liberation of souls present, past, and future.

George Bush comes out of this tumultuous endgame with high honors for charity, patience, just enough toughness, and a personal gift for diplomatic friendship to serve him well when the next crisis hit.

Drugs and dictatorship triggered the next crisis, this one in Panama, where massive narcotics trafficking created a cohort of wealthy drug lords who connived with local authorities and disdained governmental opposition. U.S. influence in the republic had waned since the canal changed hands. True, the U.S. Drug Enforcement Administration (DEA) worked hard to curtail the trade, but met varied, often ingenious, resistance, not only from the lords but also from Panama's high officials. All of which put the United States in a tough spot. DEA people and others high in the U.S. government guessed that Panama's adroit and ambitious dictator, Manuel Noriega, skimmed money from the drug trade, but he was an accommodating ally. His rise to power rested heavily on his command of Panamanian military intelligence and his personal contacts with the CIA and even the DEA. He welcomed the exiled Shah of Iran in 1979 and four years later joined in Reagan's crusade to help a fairly slippery rebel faction overthrow Nicaragua's pro-Communist government—a crusade that involved thwarting congressional mandates and sneaking funds to the rebels. As mentioned, this sordid business nearly wrecked Reagan's administration and certainly weakened the president's lengthy campaign to oust Noriega.

George Bush inherited the Panama mess; he had participated in several plans against the United States' ugly friend while he was vice president and knew that attempted coups, economic threats, and efforts to get Panamanians to clean up their country did not work. He knew Noriega as a dictator without scruple or remorse whose gangsterism stifled democracy. How to get him gone? Noriega provided the answer.

As he strengthened his power, Noriega increased his arrogance. Mixed signals from the United States permitted him to believe himself protected by his great northern ally, despite Reagan's and Bush's haphazard moves against him and a Florida court's indictment of him for drug trafficking. What the Yankees did not do was far more important than what they did. While declaiming against the dictator's obnoxious involvement in trafficking and rigging elections, several U.S. administrations had overlooked these peccadilloes. Their obsession with the Contras and Cuban information protected him. A superior sense of safety led him on. He openly violated the 1977 Panama Canal treaties and encouraged his armed forces to harass U.S. troops still in country.

All these provocations affected President Bush and his new administration. He had opposed coddling Noriega, had advocated strong measures to Reagan, and promised, during his presidential campaign, a crusade against drugs. He dawdled, though, in consulting about options, and his reputation dwindled. Was he a wimp? Did he have the strength to lead not only the United States but also the "New World Order" he had announced at the Cold War's end? Doubts about his nerve increased when the Panamanian National Assembly declared Noriega head of state on December 15, 1989, and also announced that a state of war existed with the United States. Two days later a U.S. officer was shot in Panama City, and U.S. witnesses were captured and brutalized. Noriega and his corrupt henchmen had to go. Instead of sending in the Marines in time-honored fashion, the president agreed with Gen. Colin Powell, chairman of the Joint Chiefs of Staff, and launched the massive Operation Just Cause later in the month. With the capture and elimination of the Noriega gang and preservation of order in Panama as objectives, congressional support was a given. Fourteen thousand U.S. troops went to Panama and largely achieved their objectives in a few days. There were, however, fairly many casualties, military and civilian, a host of glitches in the operation, and loud international objections. Noriega surrendered himself and is now serving a forty-year sentence in Florida.

As the first major U.S. military venture after the Cold War, Just Cause came under heavy scrutiny. Were the provocations sufficient for the response? What had gone wrong with tactics and organization to cause high losses (casualty numbers came in varieties reminiscent of the infamous Vietnam "body counts")? Why hadn't the Pentagon learned enough from Grenada to clean up its act?

Niggling, those questions were buried in surging support at home. Bush doffed the wimp image, though he had little basking time as the Middle East erupted.

Ever since the Camp David Accords in 1978, which brought a neurotic

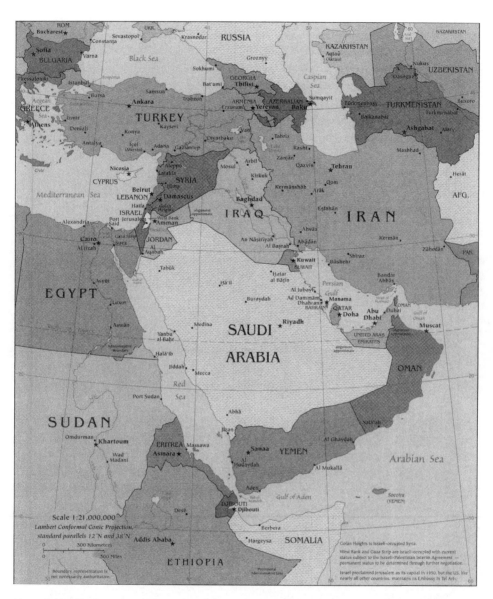

Map of Middle East, to orient readers for Iraq and environs. Courtesy of Texas A&M University Depository.

peace between Egypt and Israel, American diplomats sought to protect their puppet state as well as the oil routes to the West. This wobbling balancing act was buffeted by lingering problems with Iran and its long war with Iraq. The United States supported Iraqi leader Saddam Hussein with weapons and various other aids for at least two reasons: first, anti-Iran anger lingered from the Teheran hostage crisis and from Iran's Islamic intransigence; second, Iraq was a huge oil producer and nominally pro-Western.

Expediency, as so often happens with American policies, resulted in backing a shabby choice: at least two U.S. administrations ignored Hussein's brutal dictatorship, even his ambition to rule the Middle East, because he was an ally of convenience. Bush saw him as a gangsterly embarrassment, an opinion shared by most U.S. officials; these attitudes, though, did not translate into clear policy changes. Mixed signals or disinformation may have helped launch the Persian Gulf War.

Saddam Hussein, according to one quickly squelched news report, quizzed the U.S. ambassador about what would happen if Iraq annexed oil-rich Kuwait, and received the impression of Washington's indifference. True or not, something convinced the dictator that he could act with impunity.

On August 2, 1990, Iraqi troops stormed into Kuwait in a swiftly victorious invasion. Hussein followed up by deploying at least five divisions along the poorly defended Kuwait–Saudi Arabian border. All of which apparently stunned an unsuspecting world. President Bush fumed and knew that unpunished aggression might destabilize the world's delicate balance of peace.

James Baker, the U.S. secretary of state, happened to be visiting the Soviet foreign minister, Eduard Shevardnadze, in Irkutsk on August 2; and both discussed the new crisis. Baker wanted a joint call for an arms embargo against Iraq. Shevardnadze agreed but soon found that the longtime alliance between Baghdad and Moscow stalled quick action. Finally Shevardnadze went out on a limb and agreed. At the same time President Bush worked to build a large coalition supporting strong UN reaction — sanctions and a resolution demanding that Iraqi troops leave Kuwait. The president's hard line sprang from a certainty that naked aggression in the post–Cold War era had to be stopped. Saddam Hussein probably would not easily slink back behind his borders; he might have to be forced back. So Bush worked toward a UN ultimatum threatening war. He got it in late November 1990, after delicate negotiations with Gorbachev. Congressional approval came, but not easily—the Senate barely agreed to authorize war.

In the months after Kuwait's fall, the United States had done what it could to assure Saudi Arabia's safety. The Arab League—which represented much of the Arab world—and Britain joined Bush in gathering allies supporting the use of force. The broad coalition began sending troops to support the Saudis and a few available U.S. airborne units in Operation Desert Shield. If Hussein intended to take Saudi oil fields, he missed his chance. A swift thrust right after taking Kuwait would have succeeded easily. Probably surprised at the international reaction, he waited and watched a gathering of hosts against him.

Bush's administration faced some interesting resistance from the Pentagon. Colin Powell opposed a premature deployment of U.S. forces—his doctrine demanded overwhelming force to win in wars sustaining or securing some important national objective. There were all kinds of reasons for hanging back in Saudi Arabia: Powell wanted time for sanctions to work; the distances involved were logistically absurd—America's forward bases would be Germany and Diego Garcia. Summing up his attitude toward Middle Eastern operations, he told Secretary of Defense Dick Cheney that "the American people do not want their young dying for $1.50 a gallon oil."[1] More, the American people would not tolerate the high casualty bill coming from Iraq. Good soldier, Powell obeyed orders and began organizing massive forces in Saudi Arabia.

He had no maneuvering room. The president was implacable about Saddam Hussein. Robert Gates, a key figure among the policy makers, explained it this way: "George Bush was going to throw that son of a bitch out of Kuwait and there was never any doubt about it—regardless of what the Congress or the UN said."[2]

On January 17, 1991, Desert Shield became Desert Storm as Iraq shuddered under a smothering air barrage, and in a week the UN controlled the sky. Iraq fought back feebly with Scud surface-to-surface missiles aimed at Israel (wisely kept out of the coalition) and Saudi Arabia. With enemy power depleted from the air, UN commander Gen. H. Norman Schwarzkopf launched the ground war on February 23 with a carefully choreographed dual thrust, front and flank, by 630,000 UN troops against about 340,000 Iraqis, including the feared Republican Guard. On February 26, Baghdad announced evacuation of Kuwait as well as compliance with all UN resolutions. President Bush, urged by Powell, called off the war on February 28.

Why quit so soon, with Saddam Hussein still ensconced and lots of his army left? Obviously a continued campaign would exceed the UN mandate to free Kuwait; it would likely kill hordes of civilians beyond those already slaughtered; it would cost a good deal more in men, money, and munitions; it probably would wreck the coalition, and, as Max Boot quoted Colin Powell as saying in *The Savage Wars of Peace*, it would not make a "desert democracy where people read *The Federalist Papers* along with the Koran."[3] Vietnam's heritage really truncated the Gulf War—Vietnam's effect on General Powell.

Powell carried the baggage of defeat from a war that had slowly eroded public confidence until it nearly destroyed the Union. He recalled emotionally the media snatching defeat from victory as body bags thronged America's TV screens night after night. Media hype in Iraq threatened public support. Powell and other veterans firmly opposed the United States getting into another bloody stalemate. And if the war dragged on, it would force urban fighting with its haunts of Hue and Saigon. Not all of the Joint Chiefs were timorous, but they did agree with the Powell Doctrine: once the Iraqis were defeated, U.S. troops should come home and not sink into endless policing and guerrilla murders. With Kuwait's and Iraq's oil wells mostly saved, along with honor, Bush accepted Powell's advice, and the coalition won a grudging truce in March 1991—leaving behind buried shoots of vengeance.

What were Iraq's lessons? Mixed. The Powell Doctrine seemed valid since massive force, gathered over six months, had smashed a respected Iraqi army and done it with brutally one-sided losses (coalition killed and wounded, under 1,000, versus a guessed Iraqi 25,000; noncombat and civilian casualties not counted), and quick withdrawal prevented the nagging attrition of hostile armistice. American success with joint operations, with a high optempo backed by an arsenal of electronic warfare innovations, hinted at fundamental changes in war fighting—futuristic air war systems able to target and hit far beyond the front; long-distance air warning and intelligence from unmanned spy planes; early use of "smart" bombs; new combat and chemical clothing for ground troops; increasingly nimble command and control tools to simplify control of the battlefield now largely seen in virtual realism. These nearly miraculous tools of conquest were all designed to make war on the human cheap—casualties at last might, with a little future luck, be negated as a price for hegemony.

President Bush remarked that the Gulf War ended "the Vietnam syndrome once and for all." Not so. Ghosts from that forlorn crusade still stalk the Pentagon's halls; casualties remain anathema and haunt strategic planning.

Insecure Security

A persistent rumor dogs American military planners—that they are hostages to history and plan feverishly to fight the last war better. Witness the jibe that "military intelligence" is an oxymoron. Martial improvements seem often to take two steps back and one forward. To the extent that all service arms try to avoid repeating mistakes, this impression seems real enough. Moving a graveyard is easier than shattering shibboleths from old masters. As Barbara Tuchman drolly put it in *The Guns of August,* "nothing so comforts the military mind as the maxim of a great but dead general."[4]

Progress, though, often shades the past. Be it said for all the U.S. services, they may resist, but all American wars show that the military is not immune to innovations or to changes in environment. In the years following World War II, American military thinking opened to post–hydrogen bomb possibilities. The war validated new weaponry, as electronic warfare came nearly to dominate strategy and tactics, and helped stimulate America's scientific and technological research. Heavy casualties in Vietnam sparked special concerns with tools of remote warfare.

By the 1990s weaponry had evolved into multipurpose systems capable of controlling land, sea, and air combat zones. The Persian Gulf War not only showed the agility of the systems idea—which also revolutionized logistical concepts—but also beckoned the future by moderating or eliminating casualties. Now it seemed that what could be imagined could be produced—Reagan's Star Wars notion was antique as space became a military ecosystem. Although the Bomb remained the ultimate intimidation—especially as it spread to Third World hands—it appeared nearly dwarfed by the modern enginery of slaughter. Together these developments made the United States the most powerful nation on earth, the world's only superpower. Wherever there was trouble, America was expected to stop it.

A high hope of the Iraqi campaign had been the stabilization of the Middle East. America's quick victory and withdrawal frustrated that hope. Although his nation suffered UN embargoes and other strictures, dictator Hussein refined his repressive regime and continued his bloody campaign against the Kurdish people in northern Iraq. These outnumbered and outgunned rebels fighting for their culture and their lives appealed for help from Turkey and from the United States. Turkey feared massive Kurdish incursion along its northern border and mobilized against it. That left the United States.

President Bush realized that the Kurd allies in Desert Shield and Desert Storm had been abandoned and in April 1991 supported Operation Provide Comfort, a large humanitarian campaign to save Kurd remnants. Over 13,000 U.S. troops went to Turkey and northern Iraq. They built, organized, and often defended refugee camps while supplementing UN agencies in distributing massive amounts of medicine, food, and clothing. Much good was done and consciences were cleansed. Protective operations continued until 1996.

Humanitarian missions were nothing new to U.S. troops—they were the flip side of imperialism. American forces took relief supplies to Africa, Central and South America, Lebanon, Russia. Relief missions became an American specialty in the 1990s as troubles bubbled nearly everywhere.

Africa sizzled in postcolonial unrest; merciless feuds shattered the Balkans as the Four Horsemen kept riding in the Cold War's wake. Calls for help echoed in White House hallways, mixed with "Yankee Go Home" chants from many awash in American aid. A paraphrase of Kipling describes some of the wages of sympathy:

> Take up the leader's burden—
> The savage wars of peace—
> Fill full the mouth of Famine
> And bid the sickness cease. . . .
> Take up the leader's burden—
> And reap his old reward
> The blame of those ye better,
> The hate of those ye guard.

Fortunately, it seemed, America's efforts would blend with the UN's and so might spread the blame. Not so. America's wealth, its largesse, its sole superpower status sparked an envious anger in those it tried to help. Still, the aid kept going into a vast, insatiable maw. In the wake of the Persian Gulf War the Bush administration confronted problems in Somalia, Bangladesh, Zaire, Iraq, Saudi Arabia, Russia, and what had been Yugoslavia. Some of these problems were peacefully adjourned; others involved troop deployments and limited combat.

All these missions reflected a massive growth in America's status. From leader of the free world, the United States became the model for a global democratic urge. When William Jefferson Clinton became president of the United States in 1993 he was quickly immersed in Somalian and Haitian crises—and several lesser ones.

Clinton inherited a mess in Somalia—an unhappy pseudo-nation on the Horn of Africa. Troubles lingered there from failed U.S. and UN efforts to prevent starvation. The 1992 imbroglio sprang from nightly TV images of razor-thin, stomach-bloated children almost literally dropping dead in the streets, of emaciated parents scrab-

bling for food, of ruthless clan gangsters slaughtering supposed opponents, sometimes right in front of the cameras. Americans always respond to misery with gen-
erosity, and the public approved an administration decision to send a humanitarian
expedition into Mogadishu—which passed for Somalia's "capital."

While the public approved, the Pentagon had serious reservations. What started
as a humanitarian venture could slip into some kind of lengthy nation-building fiasco
of many casualties and few rewards. Casualties were still anathema, especially so
under media glare. Bloody pictures chilled American ardor—so it had been in Vietnam, and doubtless remained so. Some scholarly surveys challenged this idea, sug-
gesting that the public could bear more body bags than the generals; but scholars
are simply scholars, after all.

General Powell and most of his colleagues, mindful of his doctrine, wanted clear
definitions of objective, duration, and exit plans. They were straightforward enough:
take food, get in, distribute food, get out. This mission struck the generals as much
less problematic than a rumored alternative—the ethnic cleansing cesspool in former
Yugoslavia.

Since a humanitarian expedition would go, General Powell and the Pentagon
determined it would be large enough to dominate the area. Supported by a carrier
battle group and varied foreign units, a spearhead of SEAL commandos landed at
Mogadishu on the night of December 8, 1992—opposed by a large group of TV
camera crews and reporters. The skilled work of ex-ambassador Bob Oakley—
coaxed out of temporary retirement by Powell—soothed feelings of assorted warlords and produced an uneventful landing. Heavily armed Marines began quick
patrolling that stalled warlord resistance.

Powell thought the mission a success from the start. "The warlords cooperated,
and food began to flow to the countryside."[5] Ultimately some 25,000 troops supported the operation. U.S. officialdom wanted them home by Inauguration Day
1993—an increasingly impossible date as resumed feuding between warlords threatened famine once again. Objectives shifted to the Pentagon's worst nightmare—nation building, a dreaded reprise of Vietnam.

Fortunately, though, casualties were prevented by aggressive Marine patrolling.
Gradually UN forces replaced Americans and the situation degenerated. In June a
warlord's followers killed two dozen Pakistani troops and wounded fifty more. A
quick UN resolution called for finding and arresting the culpable warlord, and a
UN force, including Americans, launched a lengthy and forlorn search of Mogadishu's baffling warrens. By August the UN task force began losing men and the
Pentagon reluctantly sent Rangers and the Delta Force to keep up the hunt. On October 3, 1993, the hunted turned on the hunters, as thousands of well-armed So-
malis surrounded a Ranger and Delta Force patrol, killing eighteen, wounding
eighty-two, and capturing one soldier in the costliest day for the U.S. Army since

Vietnam. TV audiences were horrified over the next days to see American corpses dragged through the streets by cheering hordes. Although the survivors were rescued, the home front results resembled post-Tet America—the president ordered a phased withdrawal.

Powell's doctrine seemed validated one more time—and it affected many subsequent operations with the persistence of the Vietnam syndrome.

Haitian crises were old hat to Americans. White House attention focused on that unhappy land late in the nineteenth century as Yankee businessmen and bankers invested in what seemed a fairly strategic area, one lagging in commerce and money. This odd fascination persisted until a dictator was hacked to pieces in 1915. Sensitive to American expeditionary entrepreneurs, concerned, too, about possible German incursions, President Wilson sent in the Marines—and started a bitter guerrilla war. Dogged attempts to reform Haitian economics and politics failed, and by the 1930s most U.S. officials were gone.

The Cold War brought renewed Yankee interest in the bankrupt nation, as Soviet infiltration seemed possible. Reluctantly backing dictators, Washington finally settled on an apparently naïve country doctor as Haiti's president. François (Papa Doc) Duvalier was elected in 1957. Soon Haitians cringed at the appearance of his Ton Ton Macoute goon squads, which cowed the country and kept him in office. Rumor has it Haiti's Service Intelligence Nacionale (SIN), sponsor of murder squads, traded drug information to the CIA for covert support. True or not, there were death squads and terrorism under a dictatorship that beggared Castro's.

Famine and ferocity drove thousands of Haitians to flee the country. American outrage failed to faze Papa Doc. The Reagan administration tried to let him stew in the juices of rebellion but finally assisted his dethroning in 1986. An unrepentant conciliar regime was ousted in 1990 by the election of Father Jean-Bertrand Aristide, who himself was ousted by a military coup. He fled to the United States and waited for redemption.

As refugees kept flooding the United States and Haiti grew poorer than thin dirt, the UN finally approved an expedition to restore Aristide. President Clinton cooperated by ordering a naval blockade and a large invasion. Jimmy Carter, whose personal diplomacy had achieved much in North Korea, wanted to make a last-minute try for peace. President Clinton, thinking Carter "something of a wild card," agreed to negotiations about how the invasion force would be received—not whether it would go. Senator Sam Nunn of Georgia, Gen. Colin Powell, and Carter—after Munchausen-like adventures—persuaded the military junta to quit, and the landings went peacefully. Aristide returned. The Haitian peaceful invasion reflected only part of the Powell Doctrine—massive power. It violated an important corollary: Have an exit strategy. Americans once again lingered.

Much dubiety had greeted Clinton's coming, especially among hawks in and out of the military. Would this Rhodes Scholar president who dodged the draft have either the guts or the gall to use America's martial power? If Somalia and Haiti were not proof enough, other proofs came quickly.

Clinton deployed American forces far and wide in the middle and late 1990s: to South Korea, to blood-soaked Rwanda, to a still unstable Persian Gulf, to cover U.S. withdrawal from Somalia, and as reinforcements to Guantanamo. The Pentagon resisted all these ventures by citing the Powell Doctrine. A series of new Balkan crises, though, threatened multiple Vietnams.

Balkan crises seem as old as history. The socialist Yugoslavian Republic under Marshal Tito began crumbling after his death in 1980, and ancient feuds erupted. Pieces of the country sloughed into independence, and in October 1991 Bosnia-Herzegovina declared sovereignty, as did Serbia. Bosnian Serbs, backed by the largely Serbian Yugoslav Army, began a brutal ethnic cleansing campaign against the Muslim majority, the Croats, and most others in the fractured land. All of which eluded a Western glance save for the utterly callous TV cameras and the legion of reporters recording chaos.

Answering a reporter's query whether the United States could not take some limited role in Bosnia (bombing, for instance), Colin Powell restated his doctrine and preached the futility of limited wars without defined objectives and exit plans. Limited wars were like being a little pregnant—they get bigger. Powell left office in September 1993, but his influence delayed American action in Bosnia.

In 1995, when 300,000 were dead and various cities—including beautiful Sarajevo—reduced to rubble, NATO threatened heavy air strikes unless the Serbs stopped fighting. Many in the Pentagon railed against limited action, but "force protection" remained so much the command mindset that missions were scrubbed to save troops. Happily, only a few NATO (read U.S.) air raids and a Croatian offensive brought the somewhat misshapen Dayton, Ohio, peace agreement in November 1995. Air power alone had not been enough to settle the Bosnia mess, so the Powell Doctrine lingered to haunt the future.

For the Joint Chiefs of Staff the worst problem after the Cold War was the ubiquity of varied U.S. military interventions while serious pinching of military budgets shrank capabilities. Africa became a kind of staging area for air support and peacekeeping—witness various air and ground missions to Angola, Liberia, Central African Republic, Somalia, Eritrea, Guinea-Bissau, Democratic Republic of the Congo, Tanzania, Kenya, Mozambique. Diverse missions continued in the Middle East, and increasingly in the Balkans, where Bosnia seemed a mere precursor to the venom sprayed in Kosovo.

In that southernmost province of the country, Yugoslavian president Slobodan Milosevic launched a terrorist campaign to drive out the Albanian Muslim majority and restore the Serbian Orthodox Christian minority to their historic dominance. He used his largely Serbian army and assorted guerrillas to threaten, kill, burn, rape, and harass the majority into neighboring provinces. It was bloody business, and the UN ordered sanctions and finally force to end the slaughter. NATO entered the fray because it was happening in Europe.

Gen. Wesley Clark, Supreme Allied Commander in Europe (SACEUR), who would command the NATO military campaign, understood he had military problems confounded by racial, historic, religious, and Pentagon differences. He understood the Pentagon's hesitation to sink further into the Balkan ooze. As a West Point plebe he had often recited Douglas MacArthur's dictum, "There is no substitute for victory," and victory would be hard to see amid the ancient feuds and angers. Once in the Balkan wars, how to get out? These were Powell's worries and the Pentagon's. Operation Allied Force—not called a war—became the first large military effort staged by NATO. Its leaders came to see it as the first "modern war"—a euphemism for limited conflict under careful constraints. Clark, who led this melange, noted that the "highest possible technology was in use, but only in carefully restrained ways. There was extraordinary concern for military losses, on all sides."[6] Collateral damage to civilians and property was estimated—TV images in the United States might undercut the whole thing.

As with all coalition efforts, different organizations, acronyms, procedures, and languages produced nearly paralyzing confusion. Differing American martial philosophies tangled operations—the Powell school expected to fight and win wars, while an emerging minority saw peacekeeping missions as the wave of the future. High technology confounded confusion with real-time information to Washington's civilian leaders. Everyone there looked back to the 1991 Gulf War as a model—a model with little relevance to Kosovo. "For the U.S. military," Clark noted, "it was neither the conflict we had prepared for nor the war we wanted to fight."[7] But a million Albanian refugees horrified the world.

President Clinton, acting under UN and congressional agreement, approved war in March 1999. Although 28,000 allied troops were consigned to Kosovo, air power finally won what passed for victory. More than 35,000 air missions rained bombs on Serbia and Kosovo. NATO had no casualties—two planes were lost but the pilots rescued. The alliance cracked a bit with time, but held together long enough to achieve the end of fighting, the return of the refugees.

Military planners, many still charmed by the Powell Doctrine, took small comfort from the Balkans. Those campaigns pointed to science fiction wars of distant targets, precision weapons, instant information, global electronic intelligence, real-time views of multiple battlefields, unmanned aircraft, unmanned ships—even submarines—fragmented units, all remotely managed by fewer bodies. These would not be cheap wars; technology would evolve exponentially, each weapons system costlier than the last so that service procurement would escalate along with command adjustments. "Jointness," a spreading Pentagon buzzword, would mean more than service cooperation; it would encompass multinational operations. Nothing came harder than acceptance of internationalism. Winston Churchill's doubts about coalitions still resonated in Pentagon hallways, buttressed by American resistance to fighting under alien leadership.

Globalism demanded reaction, but jointness demanded different kinds of service attitudes, different professionalism as scattered brushfire wars loomed in the future. Congress, lured by budgeteering and by bulwarking civilian control of military matters, muddled the command structure by passing the Goldwater-Nichols Act in 1986. Attempting to rationalize military budgeting and unclutter the command chain, Congress created a new "joint officer specialization" that nearly sanctified joint assignments to the detriment of individual service expertise. The act also promoted the chairman of the Joint Chiefs of Staff to be the main martial adviser to Congress, the president, and the National Security Council. Arguments pro and con still rumble; some experts argue that jointness and the chairman's elevation have streamlined operations, while opponents think jointness is a distraction and that all the chiefs of staff should be in direct command of their services. There is one obvious result of the law: Pentagon and field bureaucracy have expanded beyond efficiency.

These new-fangled wars demanded not only different kinds of war fighting, but also new ways of thinking about the world. Terrorist and guerrilla conflicts would mean wars without fronts and new definitions of victory. They would also mean changing curricula at the service academies as schools shifted from a kind of lockstep antiquarianism to embrace political science, psychology, English, more foreign languages, management, even philosophy. As regime changes and peacekeeping loomed as vital functions of the army, navy, and air force, a new gender consciousness brought women into the ranks and into the academies. This change found new talents for the future but to some extent confused operations.

12

●

The Fifth Horseman

Terror antedates humanity. This Fifth Horseman stalks the food chains, abides with pestilence, lurks in war, is a wage of famine and the dread of death. It infests minds, winnows the weak, flails the strong, and at some time touches everyone. It comes in different guises with intimidation as its aim. It boasts fanatical practitioners from ancient times to the present. Xenophon's *Anabasis* speaks of psychologically hazing enemy populations. Early Roman emperors often massacred their way to the throne. Tiberius, Caligula, Nero each anchored despotism on cruelty. Rome at last fell to the terrors of Attila. Mongol conquests rested on butchery, so too Tamerlane's, Suleiman's, even Alexander's. Prisoners were the spoils of war.

On into the Dark Ages, terror's genealogy went unbroken. Religious zealotry, especially in Spain, produced the Holy Inquisition and its master of terror, Torquemada. It was, perhaps, the French who first erected terror into virtue. Speaking early in 1794, revolutionary leader Maximilien Robespierre pronounced terror as "nothing other than justice, prompt, severe, inflexible. . . . [I]t is not so much a special principle as it is a consequence of the general principle of democracy applied to our country's most urgent needs."[1] As the guillotine decimated the nation, the Académie Française defined terrorism as a "system of rule by terror."

Terrorism changed coats during the nineteenth century, becoming the tool of nongovernmental groups. Among the first was a late 1870s Russian revolutionary band called the Narodnaya Volya (People's Will). They boasted themselves terrorists, and some of their methods were templates for those to come: suffuse fear to spark revolutions and use such modern weapons as bombs and bullets for discriminating murder.

Some New World terrorists were homegrown. Pre-Columbian civilizations in Central America flourished, achieving high degrees of artistic, architectural, engineering, and mathematical skill. Differing social structures shared the fearsome primacy of priesthoods that sanctioned imperial dicta, slavery, even human sacrifice. Many warlike cultures preyed on each other, which, with sacrifice and hard living, controlled populations and superstitions. Hard living and shifting enmities made terror a Mesoamerican given.

Spanish conquistadores brought America some intimidation refinements from the Inquisition. A relatively few soldiers and friars managed native masses with genocide, torture, bondage, and racism.

As Spanish colonization moved north beyond Tenochtitlán (Mexico City) it abraded Indian tribes roaming a vast desert area. Serious fighting soon contested an advancing Spanish frontier. The plains nomads were tough, skilled with bows and horses, and with a fiendish brutality of their own. Spaniards found blood on the sand.

Northeastward in the budding American colonies, woodland Indians resisted servitude with equal demonism. Reddened woods and rivers told their skill with tomahawks, canoes, bows, and knives. Eastern and western Indian wars dogged American history to the end of the nineteenth century. Terror did not halt white expansion, but terror persisted in wars with Britain and Mexico, and finally in the bloodiest conflict of them all, the American Civil War. Terror daunted the South as Union legions followed rivers, railroads, and cavalry into almost all Confederate crannies.

One of the Civil War's many results was this return of terrorism to political uses. Under Reconstruction the South permuted into a cowed sycophancy, drained of spoils and individuality as a new and different Union began feeling pinched within its borders. Expansionism did not begin with the Spanish-American War—its roots went to Mexico and Appomattox and the heady taste of conquest.

Terror lurks in war and often makes victory hollow in an aftermath of vengeance. True enough of Yankee triumphs in Central America, Cuba, Puerto Rico, and the Philippines. Righteously committed to freeing Cuba, American imperialism marched on to make backward Filipinos ready for self-government. They, somehow, strangely resented uplifting and resisted continuing foreign occupation. As the occupation lingered, Filipino resistance escalated and skirmishes flashed through most of the islands. Resistance flickered in such southern islands as Mindanao and Jolo, home to fierce Muslim warriors. Americans themselves became adept dispensers of retributive brutality in a sputtering campaign of subjugation until World War II.

North Americans, of course, were not alone in colonial condescension. Britain, France, Germany, Italy took large slices of North, South, East, and West Africa, leaving the rest wallowing in bloody tribal wars. Britain kept a grim clutch on empire, held India by sword and governance for several generations, and fought five costly Afghan wars to little purpose. France, too, clung to the illusion of coercing Indochina into a model of Gallic culture. Italy barely held a slice of North Africa while nursing designs on Ethiopia. After the Boxer Rebellion some Western nations occupied cities on China's coast. In the late 1930s Japan attacked Chiang Kai-shek's flabby regime, unleashed terror in Nanking, and soon bogged down in distance and disdain. Colonial conflicts bred harsh terrors, often compounded by racism and improved weaponry—all grist for the Fifth Horseman's greed.

Terror kept its political/military utility in World War I and morphed with propaganda into fearful psychological dimensions as rumor passed for fact. Stories of the Rape of Belgium fanned Allied ire in 1914; rumors of bestiality wherever the Kaiser's legions went were avidly believed. Germans easily swallowed tales of British and French tortures. Terror always infested minds, but never so completely as in the Great War. There it made fiendishness real and horrors commonplace.

In Russia the Fifth Horseman scored a stellar triumph. The 1917 revolution there confirmed widespread fears of Bolshevism; terrorism ended the czars. Americans shared suspicion of Bolsheviks, and President Wilson joined an Allied effort to end the Red menace aborning by sending help to its Russian enemies. This miserably executed mission failed. Lenin, Trotsky, and company removed Russia from the war as they rammed communism down Russian throats. That began a seventy-year Reign of Terror to beggar the worst of Robespierre.

Gangster terror accompanied twentieth-century urbanization. Various mobs—notably the Mafia—waged territorial feuds, and during Prohibition in the United States, outright wars for markets piled up casualties and frightened citizens as well as police. From these conflicts came a new kind of American folk hero: Al Capone, John Dillinger, Benjamin "Bugsy" Siegel, Ma Barker and her four outlaw sons, George "Machine Gun"

Kelly, Charles "Pretty Boy" Floyd, and others won a kind of renown for bucking the system, thumbing noses at such as the G-men (the early FBI, directed against domestic terror) and local law across country.

Banditry somehow seemed to have a Robin Hood attraction for a world too long bashed by depression. It sprawled during the 1930s into terrorist mobs vying for money, power, and extortion that bloodied cities everywhere. It raged through the next decades as suicidal terrorists began blowing themselves up for varied causes. The Irish Republican Army bombed Belfast, London, and other United Kingdom cities in its continuing terror campaign for independence. Italy long suffered intrusion of the worldwide Sicilian Mafia. Many Italian political and business leaders as well as intellectuals were murdered, kneecapped, or kidnapped in the 1970s by Marxist-Leninist Red Brigades, groups intending to topple the government. Several German cities endured terrorist attacks from varied dissident groups. Beginning in 1969 a group of leftists called the Baader-Meinhof gang topped the list of fanatics. Raging until 1972, they murdered, kidnapped, bombed, and burned to take all of Germany to communism. In the late 1960s American terrorists stalked campuses and cities in protests against war and racism. Britain suffered least from terrorists—other than the IRA. During the late 1960s and early 1970s the Angry Brigade did bomb some government offices and a BBC van at the Miss World contest, but no one died; the targets were symbolic, and most of the gang had some Robin Hood credentials.

Beginning as far back as the 1930s troubles erupted in the largely British-controlled Middle East. War's end in 1945 triggered new waves of Jewish nationalism. Such terrorist bands as the Stern Gang and the Irgun bombed, executed, and frightened much of the Arab world. Pressure from them, and the likes of them, hastened British withdrawal from the Middle East and attracted attention from the United Nations. Jewish yearning for a state carved from old Palestine sparked bombings, assassinations, and torture—the terror continuing today.

Following the creation of Israel, several of its Arab neighbors fought to wreck it, and Palestinians fought for a state of their own through such well-organized terror groups as Hamas, the Palestine Liberation Organization (PLO), Hezbollah, Islamic Jihad, and others.

Middle Eastern terrorism tangled the final stages of U.S.-Soviet relations, especially in Afghanistan. There, in the late 1970s, a pro-Soviet government began disintegrating in the face of growing rebellion. The Carter administration correctly guessed that Moscow would intervene to salvage something of its considerable investment in that troubled nation. Neighboring Pakistan and even Saudi Arabia sought U.S. aid for the insurgents. Accordingly money and other "nonlethal" help went via clandestine CIA channels. A large Soviet force invaded Afghanistan on December 24 and 25, 1979, and American aid quickly jumped to billions in money, arms, intelligence, and logistical support for the Afghan Mujahedin.

Reasons were coldly logical—costly Afghan fighting might stick the USSR in a Vietnam-style quagmire of its own. That happened. For a decade the Red invaders fought the Mujahedin, climate, the mountains, disease, and frustration. Finally, tails firmly tucked, they left Afghanistan in 1988. Washington, especially under Reagan, encouraged all insurgent elements, including the Taliban and a terrorist group called Al Qaeda, financed by Washington and led by a wealthy Saudi Muslim named Osama bin Laden.

Persistent Yankee interference, efforts at reshaping a broken, wretched Muslim land, did not sit well with many former friends of convenience. Muslim wrath turned from the Soviets to all infidels. America's intrusions triggered a deep anger in Osama bin Laden's mind; the infidel United States became what he called "the Great Satan." When the Red Army left Afghanistan in 1988, the Taliban and Al Qaeda took over, and stifling religious extremists continued a toll of terror.

Oil focused most Western attention firmly on the Middle East. Within that focus Saddam Hussein's Iraq bulked increasingly large. The drastic reduction of Iraq's oil production since the Gulf War unbalanced the world's supply. That cold fact, combined with Hussein's bloody pogroms against the Kurdish and Turkish minorities, made him the ranking terrorist of the lot.

MR. BUSH'S WAR

George W. Bush, who became president in 2001, shared his father's view of Hussein and of his terrorist ties. Bush's early experience in the oil business sensitized him to the nuances of OPEC. He came into office determined to scrap America's wimp image—lingering from his father's and Bill Clinton's hesitant foreign policies—and to finish what amounted to an unfinished family crusade. From the start, he wanted Saddam Hussein gone. The question was, how?

Terror brought the answer.

On September 11, 2001, four airliners were stolen by well-trained terrorists. The first two slammed into New York City's World Trade Center towers, the third into the Pentagon, and the fourth into the ground in

Shanksville, Pennsylvania, after a heroic passenger struggle. This carefully planned attack killed some three thousand people and achieved its objective: it shattered America's dream of sanctity.

People would compare 9/11 with Pearl Harbor, some magnifying it into the biggest tragedy ever suffered by the United States. Truth be told, it ranked fairly low on American lists of disasters. Murder, roads, natural and varied catastrophes take larger tolls. The shock effect distinguished it from daily deadliness—the shock effect and the effrontery. How could a handful of "ragheads" (a pejorative term for Arabs, Muslims, and Middle Easterners) so surprise and damage the world's remaining superpower? In the wake of the attack came heroic, touching examples of citizens helping each other, of courageous firefighters and police charging into tangled ruins to save and to die.

Unreason ran rampant, as usual in post-terror anger. While most Americans knew their country was bound for increased danger, the scope, organization, the dauntlessness of the whole thing briefly unnerved the nation. President Bush stepped boldly into that uncertainty and declared war on terror. Congress agreed with the ardor of its constituents and rushed through a spate of commemorative resolutions. It passed security and enabling acts to call up reserves and to make appropriations for the terror war, and it added a shameful group of repressive acts limiting freedom of speech and communications, including the so-called USA Patriot Act of October 24, 2001, acts that skirted—if not flouted—the Constitution in a reprise of the Alien and Sedition Acts. Wars have always limited liberty, of course, but the Bush administration showed enthused interest in circumscribing American lives and liberties.[2]

At the same time, the administration, apparently bent on bravado, rather rudely shunned offered help from all allies save the British. France, Germany, and others, rebuffed, began to see a surprising aggressiveness in American actions in the Middle East.

When the president talked to Congress within a few days of the attacks, he blamed them on Al Qaeda. There seemed no connection with Saddam Hussein—and the administration began mobilizing a campaign against the Taliban and Al Qaeda in Afghanistan. Regime change was the objective: get rid of the Taliban and all the terrorists they nurtured, along with Osama bin Laden, now branded the arch terrorist.

In a tough campaign, the Taliban were soon fragmented, and a temporary government picked by the United States settled into uneasy sway over an unstable collection of religions and tribes.

Invading Afghanistan did not halt terrorism, however, and American authorities extended a search for perpetrators. Probably with a boost from the Israelis, U.S. intelligence looked toward Baghdad as the great protector of Islamic destructive gangs. Somehow Saddam Hussein transmogrified into the engineer of 9/11.

This change made sense to an administration with a festering need to cleanse the world of Hussein's sins. Varied UN sanctions had not toppled the dictator. For several long, frustrating months, Washington had confronted the UN about weapons of mass destruction (WMDs) in Iraq, presenting evidence allegedly showing that Hussein had consistently flouted UN resolutions to disarm, and that he had, in fact, clandestinely stockpiled nuclear materials nearly ready for bomb production and cached large supplies of chemical and biological warfare agents.

Irritatingly enough, persistent UN inspections belied these claims, but Hussein's stubborn noncooperation hinted at hidden weapons. President Bush knew they were there and argued that the UN should set a date for confession and renunciation. Massive antiwar feeling swept America, leaving the president atop a shrinking pyramid of support. He tried to ignore domestic opposition and pressed an attempt to build a coalition as wide as his father's in 1990–1991, but thin results rebuked the appeal. Britain— whose Prime Minister Tony Blair apparently conjured himself T. E. Lawrence redivivus—and a few other nations sent important military aid, others medical aid logistical support, some flyover permission. Some forty others voiced dilatory support for what the White House boasted as the Coalition of the Willing, and which some cynics branded the Coalition of the Bribed. The United States would, as before, carry the main burden of money, troops, air support, and modern weapons.

A reluctant UN agreed, finally, to give Saddam Hussein a short-fused deadline for giving up his WMDs. He did not. So, just after the 10:00 PM news began on the U.S. East Coast on March 19, 2003, President Bush preempted TV channels and announced that "on my orders, coalition forces have begun striking selected targets" in Iraq. Most Americans guessed it anyway, especially if they watched CNN's cameras tracking bombs in Baghdad.

Pentagon and field strategists had plotted, war-gamed, and debated throughout the winter of 2002 how to do the Gulf War better. Not only did lessons learned help, but giant steps in weapons improvement nearly made the earlier war an antique model, although Vietnam still stunted some Yankee daring. Colin Powell, now secretary of state, clung to his own doctrine about important wars: victory defined and exit secured. Technical advances created "traditional" weapons defying imagination, so advanced they could dominate battlefields and obliterate enemies.

Some highly placed Pentagoners, along with intelligence agencies, still prophesied great Iraqi military potential. A new generation of leaders, shorn of Vietnam caution, knew Iraq to be far less ready for war than it had been a decade earlier, knew, too, that a whole new generation of weapons assured victory in a modern war of terror.

American planners wrote terror into part of their offensive script. A war plan germinated in the 1990s called "Shock and Awe" would dominate the initial stages of Operation Iraqi Freedom with blanketing barrages of precision-guided missiles, "smart" blockbuster bombs, and cruise missiles coming from all directions. Such concurrent devastation should knock out Iraqi command, control, communications, and computer centers and immobilize reinforcements. War usually mangles plans, to paraphrase Moltke the Elder, and Iraq proved the point.

Targets of chance are often chancy. Just as the Shock and Awe juggernaut poised to deluge surprised Iraqi forces from everywhere, a phone rang in Lt. Gen. Michael "Buzz" Moseley's office about 1 AM (local time), March 20, 2003. Moseley, who commanded the air component of the coming tsunami, heard Chairman of the Joint Chiefs of Staff Gen. Richard Myers ask if some of his F-117s could make a pinpoint before-dawn attack on a Baghdad target. Yes. Intelligence had it that Saddam Hussein, his two sons, and other Baathist Party leaders were meeting in a downtown office complex. Pretty hard intelligence backed the request—here was an astounding target of opportunity.

Two planes did the mission, one of them equipped with two 2,000-pound bombs, the other with still more devastating ordnance. The bombs smashed into Baghdad just before dawn. Hussein and company were not where expected, and though much local damage was done, the most depressing result of the raid was revelation of an imminent attack. Secrecy blown, the impact of Shock and Awe dwindled to something less. A general invasion combining air, land, and sea action began operations from staging areas in Kuwait, the Gulf, and as far away as Diego Garcia.

In the first Bush war, service coordination came hard; this time a much smoother meshing of air, sea, and land operations pushed swiftly through forward Iraqi defenses and a two-pronged offensive swept northward on both sides of the Euphrates—a tactic completely unexpected by the enemy. Nor was the coalition strength expected either. Far from the

500,000 men collected a decade before, barely 150,000 allied troops, backed by hundreds of M1A1 Abrams tanks and clouds of fighters, bombers, helicopters, and UAVs (unmanned aerial vehicles), smashed into Iraq. Coalition army units—carefully equipped with chemical and biological protection clothing—swept on into tough desert terrain west of the storied river, a Marine Expeditionary Force raced up east of the river, and a strong British contingent moved nearly southeastward to help take Umm Kasr and then turned to Basra, where a siege developed.

Basra posed unexpected problems. With most Iraqi communications and command structures wrecked and their forces fragmented, retreating, or deserting, the Baathists in Basra clamped a firm hold on the terrified Shia—many of whom they had massacred in the Gulf War's aftermath—and organized resistance slowed British tanks, infantry, and fighting vehicles. Baath militia and irregular fedayeen fought hard, but with their T-66 tanks no match for British Challenger tanks' 120 mm guns, they were reduced to AK-47s and rifle grenades. Shrewdly refusing to be sucked into the warrens of Basra, British troops kept a loose ring around the city, let defectors defect, and slipped intelligence agents into the city for target information. Raids and snipers unnerved defenders. A highly coordinated attack on Sunday, April 6, unexpectedly routed resistance, and by day's end the few international terrorists holding the Basra University grounds were finished as the city was liberated.

Whatever hopes Hussein kept focused on Baghdad and northern areas where the Turks had refused U.S. troops entry permission. Any hope faded soon. Coalition forces spread west of the cradle of civilization—the Tigris and Euphrates areas—and left Iraqi forces almost no maneuvering room. The best efforts of the Iraqi resistance concentrated on the eastern Allied supply lines flowing toward Baghdad; sniping, suicidal raids by fedayeen, some better armed Republican Guardsmen, and Baath loyalists did disrupt logistics a bit, but two strong coalition columns closed on Iraq's capital from the east and west, and from a hastily organized mobile northern force designed not only to prevent reinforcements from the heavily Baathist Tikrit zone but also to protect the rich Kirkuk oil fields.

From the start coalition plans focused on capturing Baghdad. Although most defenses failed, soldiers and people everywhere expected a pitched battle for Iraq's inner keep. At the beginning of April a major battle erupted near the suburbs. The Iraqis fought with heavy tanks, mechanized troops, anti-aircraft guns used as field artillery, and some big guns of the Republican Guard. Routed, these defenders fled. Coalition forces edged into the city and on April 9, 2003, U.S. Marines cruised into town. Saddam's government had collapsed; rejoicing and celebration greeted the "liberators," accompanied by an occasional sniper's bullet and rocket grenades—but the main war ended.

Damage could be seen in all the major cities. Smoke clouded some of the sabotaged oil fields. And, of course, despite boasts of GPS-guided missiles and minimal damage "brilliant" bombs, there had been much collateral damage. Many civilians were killed, thousands wounded; the civil services of cities and towns were wrecked; medicine, water, and power ran short; looting flourished as law, order, and humanitarian efforts collapsed.

With Hussein's butchers gone, serious searches began for the elusive dumps of weapons of mass destruction (WMDs) that had brought the coalition together. None were found, and the searching officially ceased in December 2004.

As mentioned earlier, wars usually end messily. This one follows the emerging pattern of America's "modern wars"—it dribbled into a nation-building guerrilla foray with no discernible victory point. Simply ousting Saddam Hussein and occupying Baghdad produced a chaos of vacuity. There was celebrating among the Shias long oppressed by the Baathist ghouls, but there was also resentment of an infidel invasion seemingly aimed at Islam, bitterness at disruption of everything, anger from lingering loyalists—all of which slowly coalesced into a deliberate guerrilla campaign that hit the coalition's most delicate concern: casualties. Sniping, RPG (rifle, revolver, or rocket-propelled grenade) attacks, and ambushes began taking a small but nearly daily toll. When flag-draped caskets appeared on TV, public approval of the whole venture sagged—they rang changes on Vietnam.

As with Lyndon Johnson, a credibility gap opened between most of the American people and the president with rumors of last-minute Iraqi peace efforts deliberately ignored, as more promises and premises of the war evaporated. President Bush had promised a relatively cheap $80 billion war plus a quick campaign and swift return of the regulars and reserves called to service. But when both he and Secretary of Defense Donald Rumsfeld—hawk of the old and new schools—sent more troops and, after Baghdad's fall, asked for another $80 billion to reconstruct the destroyed nation, credibility wafted into fantasy. Worse, arrogant boasts of brilliant planning had obviously omitted some of Colin Powell's concerns—no plan existed for getting out of Iraq, and soldiers found themselves immured in counter-guerrilla actions, in civil affairs, in engineering and political and police problems they had neither expected nor been trained to do.

Obviously both the U.S. and British governments had either lied about reports of WMDs or had cynically manipulated intelligence to start the war. The Coalition of the Willing slunk to the Clutch of the Chagrined.

When, at last, there were no WMDs and fighting dragged and costs exploded, and George W. Bush announced that the United States needed to democratize the Middle East, he stood starkly revealed in the emperor's new clothes.

"Ye Shall Hear of Wars and Rumors of Wars."
—Matthew 24:6

In April 1917 President Wilson confessed to Congress that it was "a fearful thing to lead this great peaceful people into war." In a way it was a strange confession. Wars came nearly naturally to the United States from colonial times, enough to brand Yankees a warlike people. But were they and are they a militaristic people? Certainly not always. In the era of the Whiskey Rebellion, Mr. Madison's War, and Indian conflicts, Americans responded to threats, persisted with the militia system, and gave much energy to ending conflicts. Growing strength lent virtue to domestic expansion, which sparked war with Mexico—but did stabilize the Union's borders at relatively small cost in blood.

Saving the Union, then abolishing slavery, sustained the Civil War—which remains the nation's bloodiest. Again, peace was the object, and when it came, men of blue and gray finally became friends. Wars usually make their own innovations and leave things different than before. Certainly true of the Civil War, which not only annealed the Union but also beckoned the way to conquest. Although soon dissolved, the huge blue and gray legions and flotillas showed that Americans could be players in the Great Game, could, indeed, be one of the powers of the globe.

While the "military mind" is sometimes scoffed at, lessons in combined operations, new ordnance technologies, communications, logistics, and command were learned. Improvement came fairly quickly to U.S. armed forces after the Civil War and the lessons learned in Cuba, Puerto Rico, and the Philippines. Tactics shifted according to the foe. Strategy, though, suffered from uncertain political leadership. Where outcomes were obvious in Cuba, the Philippines, and the Caribbean satrapies, tactics worked well enough. Once launched into internationalism, though, the United States needed a coherent political policy shaping its military goals. And there came the rub. The United States, hungering for a voice in the world, found its new appetite at odds with traditional isolationism—hide behind the oceans and keep things close at home.

World War I temporarily interrupted isolationism. Wilson delayed taking the United States into the war, and, by the time he did, there could be no confusion about political goals. He said the war might save civilization, while nothing but all-out effort would save victory. Wilson's dream of the League of Nations foundered, and America slowly, hesitantly, learned the ways of big wars to come.

Often the twentieth century is dubbed the "American Century." More accurately, it ranks as the century of American wars: tiny wars handled by U.S. Marines intervening in, saving, or scrapping Latin American governments important to Washington; some handled by economic aid; later ones by economic/political/stealth subversion, some by terror. The century certainly had its stellar war against the Axis; a bitter UN-sponsored one without victory against Korea; and the disenchanting struggle against the Viet Cong and North Vietnam. There were small expeditions to Grenada, to Somalia, to the former Yugoslavia—these were essentially UN ventures that violated Gen. Colin Powell's emerging dynamo doctrine of combat. The first Gulf War clustered all kinds of allies in what was essentially a UN venture. It left some 300 metric tons of depleted uranium (DU) on Iraqi battlefields. DU, a deadly substance (linked to an illness plaguing many U.S. veterans, the Gulf War syndrome), has been clearly associated with genetic defects and ranks with Agent Orange in lethality. The last Gulf War scrapped all American precedents. This preemptive war without widespread public support stoked an American march to domination.

A slow process validated the march, a process often unseen or misconstrued as Americans came to feel the force of a status that conferred a burden as surely as it bestowed security—the burden of the last superpower. Suddenly global problems centered in the White House. Troubles came in the absence of an international balance of order, and the United States had the lot of world policeman apparently shoved upon it—along with all kinds of vulnerabilities. If this seemed simply random bad luck, it came from America's earlier wars building upon each other.

In a way the whole process looked ineluctable. As the United States grew stronger socially, politically, and especially economically, its international role exploded. Gradually more and more internal resources were needed to sustain the nation's opening destiny. President Eisenhower's malign "military-industrial complex," abetted by Lincoln's National Academy of Sciences, created a new power axis for the country. Industrial innovation, heavily helped by basic and applied scientific and human research from many university campuses, combined to nourish a widening imperium dictated by circumstance.

Offspring of America's earlier wars, the popular and unpopular conflicts of the twentieth and twenty-first centuries created a nearly religious national need for safety sanctified by strength and superiority. And who better than "this great peaceful people" to forge a Pax Americana?

Afterword

"War is simply power unrestrained by constitution or compact."
—William Tecumseh Sherman, 1863

Unbridled power brings unbridled corruption, along with a mesmerism to approve its ceaseless calls for more. The idea that a large army ought to be sustained fit America's emerging missionary conscience. After all, armed force would be used to spread the blessings of freedom, protect trade, manage foreign policy, and dispense the bounty of dominion. How else could all this be accomplished?

Clearly the United States could take on the world in a war. It leads in new war techniques. It certainly dominates in fancy weapons—as nearly any paperback techno-thriller shows. Books by Tom Clancy, Dale Brown, Michael DeMercurio, P. T. Deuterman, and hosts of others vie to offer the latest inventories of new tools of war, plus examples of Yankee-perfected chemical and biological agents for terror, persuasion, and plague. Not easily dismissed as fiction, these books reflect considerable personal knowledge and research by the authors. This fairly new genre shows the impact of the powerful collaboration among industry, money, and brains in refining democracy.

George Orwell would recognize today's America—as files of reservists march away to the endless terrorist wars, domestic freedom congeals; it is unpatriotic to oppose a leader, an administration struggling to keep the homeland peaceful by warring distantly, obscurely, with discerning weapons that "kill mercifully," avoid collateral damage, and almost never kill Americans! Keeping the homeland happy is not as important as keeping it docile. John Ashcroft, attorney general and a kind of minister of fear, reached back to early American history and pushed for alien and sedition legislation and emergency new laws like the Patriot Act and a sad ilk following, seized upon the horrors of 9/11 to marginalize parts of the Bill of Rights (the Fourth Amendment, prohibiting unwarranted searches and seizures, and the Sixth Amendment, guaranteeing a jury trial, a defense attorney and the right to confront accusers, and the right to be informed of the nature and cause of the accusation) and elevate President Bush above Congress—Bush, who feels a biblical zeal that those not with him are against him (Matthew 12:30)—above the law, and especially above an old American tradition of international comity, mercy, and a decent respect for world opinion.

Evidence of these Orwellian permutations are the incommunicado detainees at Guantanamo Naval Base, branded as terrorists or undesirables by executive fiat, and bound to an American Devil's Island. Especially tragic examples of a new fascism are the Iraqi victims of U.S. torture and terror at Abu Ghraib Prison.

Panic undermines a lot of things, especially law and moderation. America's current panic has permitted a new jihad, has fueled the march of imperialism, even of world domination. As panic subsides—and it seems to be fading a bit—the nation will find that the 9/11 terrorists achieved far beyond their hopes. They gave a foundering new American administration a chance for unprecedented power, a chance fundamentally to change the United States into an unsuspecting garrison state. Terrorism has always been with us; the current holy war against it is unnecessary but canny. The president's words evoked knee-jerk support rooted in deeply felt sentiments—Remember the Alamo, Pearl Harbor, the Twin Towers, Support Our Troops, Punish Terrorists.

These concerns, though, may be negated by a new kind of war being bruited by President Bush and his willing British puppet, Prime Minister Tony Blair.[1] Hints of it came with the preemptive war idea voiced by the president at West Point in June 2002: "We must take the war to the enemy. Disrupt his plans, and confront the worst threats before they emerge." In March 2003 Blair pushed the idea of a "new type of [precautionary] war" that "forces us to act even when so many comforts seem unaffected, and the threat so far off, if not illusory." Bush enhanced the idea in a TV interview: "I believe it is essential that when we see a threat, we deal with those threats before they become imminent. It's too late if they become imminent. It's too late in this new kind of war."

This "new kind of war" seems to fit Sherman's notion of unbridled power, but it goes beyond that to a kind of messianism. Blair has organized a group to identify "countries at risk of instability," and the UN is on the same trail. Obviously unstable nations will be "stabilized"—clearly a new expansion of international law. One observer sees in all this the crusades redivivus, perhaps a blueprint for precautionary wars from Korea to Syria, from Pakistan to France.

Setting things right will be difficult. President Bush's own power has pushed him to a new intolerance. To reporter Bob Woodward he remarked: "I am the commander—I do not need to explain why I say things. That's the interesting thing about being the president. Maybe somebody needs to explain to me why they say some things, but I don't feel like I owe anybody an explanation."[2] Caligula could hardly have put it better.

Congress is directed by the Constitution to share power with the executive and the Supreme Court, but since World War II Congress has retreated almost to the visitors' gallery—glib adherents of *silent leges inter arma!* Members of both houses should reread the Constitution and remember that they are sworn to protect and defend it against *all* enemies, foreign and domestic. They have elided the meaning of the war declaration power by group consultations with the president, and open approval of military action without specific controls has been the result: the Tonkin Gulf Resolution, the early October 2002 resolution giving the president personal authority to make war. Congress also would do well to recall that they hold the power of the purse: they can cut off illegal wars; they can scale back bankruptcy. They should ponder most seriously Jefferson's dictum that "when the government fears the people, there is liberty, when the people fear the government, there is tyranny."[3]

Congress might also remember James Madison's 1793 comment on Article I, Section 8 of the Constitution, which gives Congress the power to declare war: "In no part of the Constitution is more wisdom to be found than in the clause which confides the question of war or peace to the legislature, and not the executive department." Maybe that article and section should be amended to include specifically the phrase "and make peace." This might terminate presidential efforts at wayward nation meddling.

Since Roman precedents stalk America's present, it might be useful for Congress to revive the idea of a six-month dictator for the prosecution of war. Out at the end of six months, the dictator returns to civil life. If war continues, more dictators could be found, always facing a truncated official future and a brake on ambition.

In planning for new-style wars ahead, Congress might consider a similar six-month moratorium on pork-barrel appropriations. It might take a more serious interest in the Pentagon's needs and not force local fancies on military experts. A good deal of money and respect is lost when Congress arrogates technical and battle knowledge to the level of its incompetence. For its part, the Pentagon must not focus so exclusively on getting over the lessons of Vietnam that it forgets the lessons of World War II. The United States has generated so many recent enemies that a large coalition against it is not impossible, nor is a large war.

Behind all this is a basic possibility: that things have drifted nearly beyond redemption. Has the United States already sold itself out to the endless maw of militarism? Some foreign observers see the United States in a periodic state of madness, as in the days of A. Mitchell Palmer and Joseph McCarthy. Those dangerous times faded with a return to national reason. But has the nation willingly accepted an unconstitutional monarchy and passed through the time of democracy into the pigsty of tyranny? Has it looked at its erstwhile enemies and found itself a rogue state terrorizing the world in the name of values it no longer embodies? Is the spoor of its imperialism—military bases bestrewn around the globe—proof of a drive to domination?

Is America finished? The final verdict lies with the American people. Optimism, care for the underdog, and a deep-struck love of liberty run through the nation's blood and history, through its wars and its times of peace. While it may seem that presentism currently mixed with imperialism has destroyed what passed for the American mind, a slowly spreading countrywide alarm about the future hints at the rise of a mature American national conscience—a conscience that defeated British tyranny, saved the Union, fought to make the world safe for democracy, joined a crusade against fascism, and underwrote the fall of the USSR, a conscience that is still abroad in the land.

It may be that an old Yankee anger will rise up to America's greatest crisis yet, take aim at the future, and prove that "man's last best hope of freedom" has not perished but only consigned one more pretender to the laughter of history.

Notes

THE WHISKEY REBELLION

1. May 2, 1792, Militia Act, in *The Public Statutes at Large of the United States of America*, edited by Richard Peters, 8 vols. (Boston, 1845–1846), 1:264–266.

2. *Pennsylvania Archives*, edited by Samuel Hazard et al. (Philadelphia and Harrisburg, 1852–1949), 2nd ser., 4:122–124.

3. Diary entry for October 6–12, 1794, in *The Papers of George Washington: Diaries*, vol. 6, January 1790–December 1799, edited by Donald Jackson et al. (Charlottesville: University Press of Virginia, 1979).

4. Quoted in Dave R. Palmer, *1794: America, Its Army, and the Birth of the Nation* (Novato, CA: Presidio Press, 1994), 273.

5. Quoted in ibid., 275.

MR. MADISON'S WAR

1. James Madison to Thomas Jefferson, April 2, 1798, in *The Writings of James Madison*, edited by Gaillard Hunt (New York: G. P. Putnam's Sons, 1906), 6:312.

THE WAR WITH MEXICO

1. James M. Drake, quoted in *The Oxford Companion to American Military History*, edited by John W. Chambers (New York: Oxford University Press, 1999), 481.

THE CIVIL WAR

1. Abraham Lincoln to Lyman Trumbull, December 10, 1860, quoted in Reinhard Henry Luthin, *The Real Abraham Lincoln* (Englewood Cliffs, NJ: Prentice-Hall, 1960), 242.

2. Abraham Lincoln to Horace Greeley, August 22, 1862, in *The Collected Works of Abraham Lincoln*, edited by Roy P. Basler (New Brunswick, NJ: Rutgers University Press, 1955), 5:388.

THE SPANISH-AMERICAN WAR

1. Max Boot, *The Savage Wars of Peace: Small Wars and the Rise of American Power* (New York: Basic Books, 2002), 162.

THE SECOND WORLD WAR

1. Inscribed on the World War II Memorial, Washington, DC.

KOREA

1. Harry S. Truman, *Memoirs*, vol. 2, *Years of Trial and Hope* (Garden City, NY: Doubleday, 1956), 463.

2. Maurice Matloff, gen. ed., *American Military History* (Washington, DC: Office of the Chief of Military History, U.S. Army, 1969), 574.

3. Author's interview with John B. Connally, Austin, Texas, September 9, 1991.

THE COLD WAR

1. Quoted in Dinesh D'Souza, "How the East Was Won," *American History* 38, no. 4 (2002): 40–41.

2. Ibid., 39.

NEW WAR, OLD COST

1. Quoted in Boot, *Savage Wars*, 320.

2. Robert M. Gates, *From the Shadows: The Ultimate Insider's Story of Five Presidents and How They Won the Cold War* (New York: Touchstone, 1996), 499.

3. Boot, *Savage Wars*, 321.

4. Barbara Tuchman, *The Guns of August* (New York: Bonanza, 1982), 19.

5. Colin Powell with Joseph E. Persico, *My American Journey* (New York: Ballantine Books, 1995), 551.

6. Wesley K. Clark, *Waging Modern War: Bosnia, Kosovo, and the Future of Combat* (New York: Public Affairs, 2001), xxiv.

7. Ibid., 19.

THE FIFTH HORSEMAN

1. Maximilien Robespierre, "On the Moral and Political Principles of Domestic Policy," speech delivered February 5, 1794.

2. For a sharp legal attack on civil liberty restriction under Bush and Attorney General John Ashcroft, see R. Dworkin, "Terror and the Attack on Civil Liberties," *The New York Review of Books*, November 6, 2003. Dworkin is a law professor at both New York University and Oxford University.

AFTERWORD

1. See Michael Byers's excellent article, "A New Type of War," *London Review of Books*, May 6, 2004, 27–28.

2. Bob Woodward to interviewer Mike Wallace, November 17, 2002, quoted in "A Rare Glimpse Inside Bush's Cabinet," http://www.cbsnews.com/stories/2002/11/17/60minutes/printable529657/shtml.

3. Quoted in Chalmers Johnson, "Sorrows of Empire," 6, Foreign Policy in Focus, http://www.irc-online.org.

Further Reading

Ambrose, Stephen A., with original text by C. L. Sulzberger. *American Heritage New History of World War II*. New York: American Heritage, 1997.

Bell, William Gardner. *Secretaries of War and Secretaries of the Army—Portraits and Biographical Sketches*. Washington, DC: Center of Military History, U.S. Army, 1982.

Boot, Max. *The Savage Wars of Peace: Small Wars and the Rise of American Power*. New York: Basic Books, 2002.

Catton, Bruce, James M. McPherson, and Noah A. Trudeau, eds. *The American Heritage New History of the Civil War*. New York: Viking Press, 1996.

Chambers, John Whiteclay, ed.-in-chief. *The Oxford Companion to American Military History*. New York: Oxford University Press, 1999.

Clark, Wesley K. *Waging Modern War: Bosnia, Kosovo, and the Future of Combat*. New York: Public Affairs, 2001.

Coffman, Edward M. *The Old Army: A Portrait of the American Army in Peacetime, 1784–1898*. New York: Oxford University Press, 1986.

Commager, Henry S., and Milton Cantor, eds. *Documents of American History*. 2 vols. Englewood Cliffs, NJ: Prentice Hall, 1988.

Fitzgerald, Francis. *Fire in the Lake: The Vietnamese and the Americans in Vietnam*. New York: Vintage, 1989.

Gates, Robert M. *From the Shadows: The Ultimate Insider's Story of Five Presidents and How They Won the Cold War*. New York: Touchstone, 1996.

Karnow, Stanley. *Vietnam: A History*. New York: Viking, 1983.

Matloff, Maurice, gen. ed. *American Military History*. Washington, DC: Office of the Chief of Military History, U.S. Army, 1969.

Murray, Williamson, and Robert H. Scales, Jr. *The Iraq War: A Military History*. Cambridge, MA: Belknap Press of Harvard University Press, 2003.

Nelson, William H., and Frank E. Vandiver. *Fields of Glory: An Illustrated Narrative of American Land Warfare*. New York: E. P. Dutton, 1960.

Palmer, Dave R. *1794: America, Its Army, and the Birth of the Nation*. Novato, CA: Presidio Press, 1994.

Ridgeway, Matthew B. *The Korean War*. New York: Doubleday, 1967.

Vandiver, Frank E. *Blood Brothers: A Short History of the Civil War*. College Station, TX: Texas A&M University Press, 1995.

———. *Shadows of Vietnam: Lyndon Johnson's Wars*. College Station, TX: Texas A&M University Press, 1997.

Weigley, Russell F. *The American Way of War: A History of United States Military Strategy and Policy*. New York: Macmillan, 1973.

———. *History of the United States Army*. New York: Macmillan, 1967.

Index

About the Author

FRANK E. VANDIVER was Distinguished University Professor, President Emeritus of Texas A&M University, and Director of the Mosher Institute for Defense Studies. He was Professor of History and Provost of Rice University. He held the post of Harmsworth Professor of American History at Oxford University and taught at the United States Military Academy. His books include *Black Jack: The Life and Times of John J. Pershing* (National Book Awards Finalist); *Mighty Stonewall*; *Shadows of Vietnam: Lyndon Johnson's War*; and *Their Tattered Flags: The Epic of the Confederacy*.